READING SKILLS AND STRATEGIES
REACHING STRUGGLING READERS

Reading Strategies Handbook
FOR MIDDLE SCHOOL

ELEMENTS OF Literature

A GUIDE TO TEACHING READING
IN THE LITERATURE CLASSROOM

by Dr. Kylene Beers
University of Houston
with a foreword by Robert E. Probst

HOLT, RINEHART AND WINSTON
Harcourt Brace & Company
Austin • New York • Orlando • Atlanta • San Francisco • Boston • Dallas • Toronto • London

Staff Credits

Associate Director: Mescal Evler
Manager of Editorial Operations: Robert R. Hoyt
Managing Editor: Bill Wahlgren
Executive Editors: Katie Vignery, Patricia A. McCambridge
Project Editor: Victoria Moreland
Component Editor: Pamela Thompson
Editorial Staff: *Assistant Managing Editors,* Amanda F. Beard, Marie H. Price; *Assistant Editor,* Chi Nguyen; *Copyediting Manager,* Michael Neibergall; *Senior Copyeditor,* Mary Malone; *Copyeditors,* Joel Bourgeois, Gabrielle Field, Suzi A. Hunn, Jane Kominek, Millicent Ondras, Theresa Reding, Désirée Reid, Kathleen Scheiner; *Editorial Coordinators,* Marcus Johnson, Mark Holland, Robert Littlefield, Jill O'Neal, Tracy DeMont; *Assistant Editorial Coordinators,* Janet Riley, Summer Del Monte; *Support Staff,* Lori De La Garza, Pat Stover, Matthew Villalobos; *Word Processors,* Ruth Hooker, Margaret Sanchez, Kelly Keeley, Elizabeth Butler, Gail Coupland

Research and Development: Joan Burditt

Permissions: Tamara A. Blanken, Ann B. Farrar
Design: *Art Director, Book Design,* Richard Metzger; *Design Manager, Book & Media Design,* Joe Melomo
Prepress Production: Beth Prevelige, Simira Davis, Sergio Durante
Media Production: *Production Manager,* Kim A. Scott; *Production Coordinator,* Belinda Barbosa; *Production Supervisor,* Nancy Hargis
Manufacturing Coordinators: Michael Roche, Belinda Barbosa

Copyright © by Holt, Rinehart and Winston

All rights reserved. No part of this publication may be reproduced or transmitted in any form or by any means, electronic or mechanical, including photocopy, recording, or any information storage and retrieval system, without permission in writing from the publisher.

Requests for permission to make copies of any part of the work should be mailed to the following address: Permissions Department, Holt, Rinehart and Winston, 1120 South Capital of Texas Highway, Austin, Texas 78746-6487.

For permission to use copyrighted material, grateful acknowledgment is made to the following sources:

Christopher-Gordon Publishers, Inc.: Appendix 5.B from *Into Focus: Understanding and Creating Middle School Readers,* edited by Kylene Beers and Barbara G. Samuels. Copyright © 1998 by Christopher-Gordon Publishers, Inc.

Nelson ITP: Figure 3.14 (comparison grid) from *Literacy Through Literature,* by Terry D. Johnson and Daphne R. Louis. Copyright © 1987 by Terry D. Johnson and Daphne R. Louis.

Printed in the United States of America

ISBN 0-03-054862-4

TABLE of CONTENTS

FOREWORD v

INTRODUCTION 1

STRATEGIES

    Anticipation Guides 17

    It Says…I Say 25

    Most Important Word 35

    Probable Passage 43

    Retellings 49

    Save the Last Word for Me 57

    Say Something 65

    Scales 73

    Sketch to Stretch 81

    Somebody Wanted But So 91

    Story Impressions 99

    Text Reformulation 107

    Think-Aloud 115

    Vocabulary Development 125

READING STRATEGIES AT A GLANCE 139

BIBLIOGRAPHY 143

Foreword

by
Robert E. Probst
Professor of English Education, Georgia State University

Reading is a mysterious process for most of us. Who knows how it happens, or how we do it? We pick up a book, flip open to the first page, stare at the print, and images form in our minds. People are conjured out of ink and paper, and events of centuries ago are recreated, happening once again in some strange space that seems to be at once in our thoughts and out in the world. Events that never happened—and never could—transpire with more vitality and impact than yesterday's actual happenings. Thoughts come to us, questions arise, emotions are stirred—all in the simple act of looking at ink on paper. Like breathing or walking, we just do it, without thinking much about how.

Yet reading isn't so simple, natural, and easy for all of us. Some readers stare at the ink on paper and see, well, ink on paper. Or they see the words, and can even speak those words aloud, but as they do, little happens in their minds. Images don't form, questions don't arise, and emotions aren't stirred. In such reader's minds, characters don't walk across a stage, but rather stand unmoving like unadorned department store mannequins—if, indeed, they take any shape at all.

For us to help those readers, we must steal some of the mystery from the process of reading. We need to look closely at what happens so naturally—almost unconsciously—for some of us, so that we may teach reading to those readers for whom this process comes less naturally. The characters in a book don't, after all, just get up and march as we stare at the page. We do something to make them perform for us. We work—easily and instinctively if we are lucky, or with conscious effort and some labor if we are not—to see the people described for us, to conjure in our imaginations the events depicted for us, to question and analyze the ideas presented to us. Despite the deceptively quiet immobility of the entranced reader, motionless in his or her chair except for the periodic turning of pages, reading is an active process. It involves doing things—engaging in specific, describable, teachable acts.

As teachers, we haven't always taught reading. Too often, we've assigned it and expected it and tested it. In this *Reading Strategies Handbook*, Kylene Beers has written about some of those specific, describable, teachable acts of which reading consists. Kylene's years of work with readers—some of whom are enthusiastic, some reluctant, some downright hostile to both books and teachers—has yielded a set of strategies, usable and practical, that will help teachers initiate readers more successfully and happily into the pleasures of reading. The *Reading Strategies Handbook* is an attempt to help all of us instruct our students more successfully, so that all of them may someday enjoy the mysteries of books.

Robert E. Probst established the pedagogical framework for the 1997 and 2000 editions of *Elements of Literature*. He is the author of *Response and Analysis: Teaching Literature in Junior and Senior High School*. He has also contributed chapters to such books as *Literature Instruction: A Focus on Student Response*; *Reader Response in the Classroom: Evoking and Interpreting Meaning in Literature*; and *For Louise M. Rosenblatt*. Dr. Probst is a member of the National Council of Teachers of English and has worked on the council's Committee on Research, the Commission on Reading, and the Commission on Curriculum. Dr. Probst has also served on the board of directors of the Adolescent Literature Assembly and is a member of the National Conference on Research in Language and Literacy.

INTRODUCTION

Reaching Struggling Readers: A Teacher's Journey to Understanding

by Dr. Kylene Beers

A Journey Begins

The well-dressed parents, the assistant principal, and I all sat in the conference room of the middle school where I taught. The parents looked at me expectantly as the mother asked, "Can you tell us what Ben's reading problem is?"

After a moment of thought, I replied, "He's having trouble understanding what he reads."

They nodded. And waited. So I continued, "I'd say it's a comprehension problem."

A flicker of something—disappointment, confusion, anger?—appeared on the father's face.

"Well, I suppose if he can't understand what he's reading, then that would be a comprehension problem," he said. His wife nodded. The assistant principal nodded. I nodded. We all sat there nodding. I hoped that that meant the parent-requested conference was now over. But then Ben's father stopped nodding. So did his wife. "As a matter of fact," he continued, "I knew before we came in here that Ben has problems with comprehension. What my wife and I want to know from you, his teacher, is this: Just what is his comprehension problem, and what do you plan to do to help him correct it?"

I began to sweat because I didn't know the answer to his question. I was a secondary English teacher with all of one year of teaching experience. When I had chosen to teach adolescents, I had assumed that they'd already know how to read. I had imagined spending class time discussing protagonists and antagonists, symbolism and imagery. We were going to have rousing debates about theme, critically addressing our own interpretations of the text. I wasn't an elementary teacher, so I didn't expect or particularly want to teach reading. I was a *literature* teacher. I didn't have a clue why Ben couldn't comprehend what he read, and I certainly had no specific thoughts about what to do.

I finally mumbled something about watching him closely and getting back with them later. Ben's parents left knowing what I knew—I didn't know how to help their son.

I failed as a teacher for Ben that year because I didn't really teach him what he most needed to know. I continued to be the literature teacher I wanted to be, and when Ben couldn't understand the stories in our anthology or our class novels, I either asked what his elementary teachers had been doing or wondered what was wrong with Ben.

But Ben didn't fail me. He did what students so effortlessly do: He showed me what I didn't know and gave me a reason to learn those things. Thus began my transformation from literature teacher to literature/reading teacher. Ben helped me to become one of those teachers who believes that it is never too late to help students learn comprehension and decoding strategies, and who also believes that if we allow our students to leave high school with either an inability to read or an antipathy toward reading, then we have failed them and failed them miserably.

The journey that began with Ben has consumed my now twenty years of being an educator. It has sent me back for graduate degrees, taken me into elementary and high school classrooms, kept me talking with students and teachers, and inspired me to look constantly for ways that I, a literature teacher, can help teens learn to read and like to read.

Though Ben started me on my journey, it was another student, Al, who provided the direction.

On the Journey: Figuring Out Where to Go

My third-period English class during my third year of teaching was going great—or so I thought. During the summer I had found an old reading textbook and had made myself a list of reading skills that the book said all readers needed. I had decided that I was just going to march my students through each of those skills as we read our literature book, and then they would be better readers.

On this particular day, I had written the daily objective on the board ("The learner will find the main idea in a text") and had told the students that this week we'd be reading a story in our literature books and then discussing the main idea. To get ready for that, we'd first read some paragraphs on a worksheet and find the main idea there. I then distributed the freshly mimeographed pages and read the directions to the students: *Read each of the following paragraphs. After each paragraph, read each series of statements and circle the one that is the main idea of the paragraph.*

"Okay?" I said. "Remember to read carefully so you can find the main idea." (That was the extent of my instruction. I think I had managed to confuse "instruction" with "instructions." But that's another journey.)

Twenty-seven heads bent down as students began reading. I returned to my desk to catch up on some grading. Then Al, the new student from the fifth seat, fourth row, appeared at my desk.

"Yes, Al?" I asked.
"What do I do?" he asked, pointing at the sheet.
"Did you read the directions?" I responded.
He nodded.
"Okay. Well, did you read the first paragraph?" I asked.
He nodded again.
"Okay. So, now you read these options and choose the main idea." I said.
"But how do I know what the main idea is?" he asked.
"What? The main idea is, well, the idea that is the main one. The most important one."
"Yeah, but how do I know what that is if I don't already know what the main idea is?"

How do I know if I don't already know? I thought about Al's words for a long time after he had returned to his seat to guess at answers. For weeks, I stared at that worksheet and lots of others before I finally understood what he was talking about. That worksheet could be completed by the twenty or so students in the room who already understood how to figure out the main idea of a passage. But for the students who didn't already understand what the main idea was, the worksheet didn't help them. More importantly, neither did I.

At the Intersection of Skills and Strategies

My growing suspicion of skill-based instruction made me wonder if I didn't believe in skills. *Skills* was beginning to be a somewhat unpopular word about this time, somehow implying that, if you believed in them, then it meant your classroom was worksheet-driven and drill-laden, and your teaching was outdated. Yet I couldn't ever let go of the fact that I not only believed in so-called reading skills, but used those skills myself. So how could I not believe in skills?

Although I couldn't let go of the skills, I also couldn't deny that I was seeing more and more students like Al—students who didn't seem to be able to do the skill exercises I gave them to do. *How do I know if I don't already know?* I slowly began to understand that for students who could generalize, analyze, make connections, make predictions, see causal relationships, keep events in sequence, and so forth, the worksheets that called for them to practice those skills were simply that: practice. But for students who couldn't do those things in the first place, the worksheets were just another opportunity for failure, not a vehicle for learning.

I began to rethink how I was teaching. Outside my classroom, I began taking reading courses at the university. I started studying the psychology of reading and the reading process. I began reading texts by folks like Frank Smith and Louise Rosenblatt and Ken Goodman and Marie Clay and Robert Probst. Inside my classroom, I stopped using worksheets that were nothing more than skill practice sheets. I made a list of what my district at that time identified as the reading skills students had to master: comparing and contrasting, making predictions, drawing conclusions, forming inferences, determining the main idea, sequencing, forming opinions, summarizing, and finding cause-and-effect relationships.

Then I asked myself how to get from point A (for example, the student can't summarize) to point B (the student can summarize). To answer that question, I first had to understand just what kind of thinking students had to be able to do in order to summarize. It seemed to me that, among other things, students had to be able to sequence. They had to be able to analyze, synthesize, and evaluate, and even to compare and contrast.

Next, I had to determine if students could actually think analytically (or sequentially, or comparatively), because somewhere along the way I had come to understand that reading skills are simply thinking skills applied to a reading situation. Was the problem that kids couldn't analyze, couldn't evaluate, couldn't classify? Or did they simply not know how to do those things in a reading situation?

To find out, I began listening to students talk and recording what they said about their lives. I kept countless anecdotal notes. I was not so much interested in what the students were saying, but rather in the type of thinking that was revealed through their conversations. The following brief exchange between Jenny and Callie, two struggling readers, turned out to be instructive:

Jenny: Saw you at the dance last night.
Callie: Yeah, it was pretty good, except the decorations. They were dorky.
Jenny: Yeah, we ought to have a new decorations committee. The ones from last year were so much better than this year.
Callie: Ya think so? How come?
Jenny: Remember those balloon arch things and all the stuff on tables? We didn't have any of that stuff this year. And remember how when we arrived we all first had to walk under the arches, then like through a tunnel thing and then finally we were on the dance floor? That was really cool.

As I listened to this dialogue, I saw what the skill activity sheets weren't showing me: Jenny could analyze, synthesize, and evaluate. She could compare and contrast, sequence, and summarize. She could do the thinking; she just didn't see how to connect the type of thinking she could do to a reading situation. What she lacked was a strategy, or a scaffold, that could provide the framework for the thinking skills she needed to apply to her reading.

I began trying out a variety of strategies with students to see how strategies and skills intersected. I wasn't the only one looking at strategic thinking; a great deal has been written about it (see references at the end of this chapter for what others have written about strategies). I, like many others, had discovered that teaching students specific strategies gave them a vehicle for getting to the thinking skills they already possessed but just hadn't figured out how to use in a reading context.

Reading strategies can create a learning environment that encourages certain types of thinking. The following chart shows how the various reading strategies in this handbook can be effectively linked to specific reading skills.

Reading Skill	Reading Strategy	When Can I Use This Strategy?		
		Before Reading	During Reading	After Reading
Analyzing cause and effect	Text Reformulation Semantic Differential Scales Somebody Wanted But So	 X 	 X 	X X X
Analyzing chronological order	Retellings			X
Analyzing persuasive techniques	Anticipation Guides Save the Last Word for Me	X 	X 	X X
Comparing and contrasting	Anticipation Guides Semantic Differential Scales	X X	X X	X X
Drawing conclusions	It Says...I Say Save the Last Word for Me Sketch to Stretch		X 	X X X
Establishing a purpose for reading	Anticipation Guides Probable Passage Story Impressions	X X X	X X	X X X
Identifying the main idea	Most Important Word Retellings			X X

Reading Skill	Reading Strategy	When Can I Use This Strategy?		
		Before Reading	During Reading	After Reading
Making generalizations	It Says...I Say		X	X
	Most Important Word			X
	Sketch to Stretch			X
Making inferences	It Says...I Say		X	X
Making predictions	Anticipation Guides	X	X	X
	Probable Passage	X		X
	Story Impressions	X	X	X
Monitoring reading	Say Something		X	
	Think-Aloud		X	
Summarizing	Most Important Word			X
	Somebody Wanted But So			X
Understanding text structure	Text Reformulation			X
Using prior knowledge	Anticipation Guides	X	X	X
	Say Something		X	

Because they promote many different kinds of thinking, reading strategies are inherently flexible and adaptable. As you study the chart, you'll notice that I use multiple strategies to help students master the same skills. For instance, if I see that students need help in making generalizations, I can use the It Says . . . I Say strategy, (page 25), Most Important Word (page 35), or Sketch to Stretch (page 81). In the same way, each strategy can be used to teach a multitude of reading skills. For instance, the Anticipation Guides strategy can be used to help students make predictions, compare and contrast, establish a purpose for reading, analyze persuasive techniques, and use prior knowledge, among other skills.

The chart is by no means exhaustive. After reading this handbook, you may decide to adapt strategies to help your students practice different skills or additional skills not listed on this chart. I'm constantly looking for additional ways to help students make predictions, paraphrase, or determine the main idea of a selection. But for now, this handbook features the strategies that I have found most successful in eliciting certain reading (or thinking) behaviors in students.

While making my journey from skills to strategies, I stumbled upon many issues that sent me on side trips. In particular, I wondered how strategy instruction looks in a classroom, whether strategy instruction helps all readers, how assessment works, and whether strategies could encourage reluctant readers to read.

Side Trip #1: Strategies at Work

Belinda, a student in the tenth grade, was having trouble writing summaries. Her teacher told me that Belinda's attempts at summary-writing were either much too vague ("It's about a girl and she gets lost and then gets found") or much too detailed (three pages of hand-written notes filled with "And then this happened"). The teacher wanted a succinct summary that mentioned a character or two, something important that happened, some conflict, and a resolution, but Belinda couldn't produce it.

To help Belinda write the type of summary her teacher wanted, I taught her a strategy called Somebody Wanted But So (page 91), a strategy that other teachers had taught me. After reading a selection from her literature book, Belinda discussed with me who she thought the most important *somebody* in the story was. Next, she told me what that somebody *wanted*. Then she went on to explain the *but*: something happened to that somebody, making it difficult to achieve what that character wanted. Finally, Belinda identified the *so*: how that character solved the problem and what eventually happened to the character.

Read the following transcript of the dialogue we had after Belinda finished reading the short story "Poison" by Roald Dahl. You'll see that Belinda, when given the Somebody Wanted But So strategy, could do the thinking necessary for creating a summary.

Somebody	Wanted	But	So

Belinda: The somebody I want to talk about? Well, I guess that would be the man who had the snake on him, Harry.

KB: Okay. Now look at the chart and tell me what you need to do next.

Belinda: I have to say what Harry wanted? Okay. Well, he was in bed and this snake crawled up the bed and got on his stomach. It was a really poisonous one, and he couldn't move and so he wanted his friend, um, Timber, to help him.

KB: Okay. Now what do you do?

Belinda: Um, say but what happened? Well, Timber, that was his friend, he wasn't sure what to do so he got the doctor and then they tried to

	put the snake to sleep with that cho-chl- [chloroform] — well, with some stuff you use to put things to sleep.
KB:	And now what?
Belinda:	Um, I tell so what happened. Okay. Well, they did that and then they pulled back the covers and looked and there wasn't any snake. Harry got embarrassed and mad at the doctor.
KB:	Now, put the whole thing together. *[I had taken notes, putting her comments into the correct columns as she talked. Now I gave her the notes.]*
Belinda:	*[Belinda spent two or three minutes looking at the notes. Then she grinned and began.]* Harry was in bed and this snake crawled up the bed and got on his stomach. It was a really poisonous one, and he couldn't move and so he wanted his friend, um, Timber to help him. But Timber, his friend, wasn't sure what to do so he got the doctor and then they tried to put the snake to sleep with some stuff you use to put things to sleep. So after they did that, they pulled back the covers and looked and there wasn't any snake. Harry got embarrassed and mad at the doctor.

Instead of simply asking Belinda to summarize the story, which had proven to be an ineffective approach, I gave her a strategy. That strategy provided a scaffold, enabling Belinda to work through a process whose product was a summary. Eventually, after using the strategy successfully many times, Belinda no longer had to use Somebody Wanted But So because she had internalized the process. She was able to create the product (a summary) without the scaffold.

Side Trip #2: Strategies and Students: Who Benefits?

Strategies help all learners, not just struggling ones. Skilled readers are skilled, in part, because they understand how to make sense of texts. They know how to apply all those things we call reading skills without having to work through the process of a strategy. But less-skilled readers need the scaffold a strategy provides.

Less-skilled readers often think that skilled readers simply open a book, let their eyes fly over words, and then understand all there is to understand. Struggling readers don't see all the cognitive processes that skilled readers use to make meaning. They don't see the rereading, the inferencing, the generalizing, the connecting, the comparing, the predicting, the sequencing. They just see that certain kids always seem to know the right answers. Surely, it must be magic! Or, as Eric once said to me: "Those kids, the ones that always know the answers, it's because they are just good readers." "What makes them good readers?" I asked. "Knowing the answers," he replied. So, according to Eric's circular reasoning, good readers know the answers and they know the answers because they are good readers. I asked Eric if he thought good readers were good because they did things like make inferences or make connections. His response—"Huh?"—spoke volumes.

Then Eric began an intense several months of learning and using the strategies Retellings, Say Something, Think-Aloud, Somebody Wanted But So, and It Says . . . I Say. After four months he told me that he "never knew there was so much thinking that went on with reading."

Students like Eric will benefit the most from the strategies presented in this handbook. I've used most of these strategies, however, with all levels of students. I find that gifted students particularly enjoy Most Important Word (page 35) and Sketch to Stretch (page 81). Well-crafted Anticipation Guides (page 17) offer verbal students rich discussion opportunities. Semantic Differential Scales (page 73) also give verbal students a chance to explain their beliefs about characters, while Text Reformulation (page 107) allows them to exercise creative thinking.

When trying to decide which strategy to use with a particular student, I always ask myself how the strategy benefits the student. If the only benefit is that the student gets practice with a skill he or she already possesses, then I don't use the strategy.

Side Trip #3: Strategies and Assessment: An Important Connection

When you're using strategies, there are three types of assessments to consider. First, you need to assess whether or not the strategy is resulting in the types of reading skills (thinking skills) the student needs. Second—though this is not applicable to all strategies—you need to assess the quality of the product that results from some strategies. (For instance, Text Reformulation results in a written product.) Third, you need to provide students with the opportunity to assess their own use of a particular strategy.

Let's look at the first area of assessment—checking to see if the strategy is resulting in the reading/thinking behaviors students need. In one tenth-grade class, the students used the Say Something strategy (page 65) as they read a poem. This strategy requires that students read something with a partner, stopping at various points throughout the text to say something specific. Students can make predictions, make comments, ask questions, or make connections. We chose specific places in the poem where they would stop to say something, and then the students began reading. While they were reading, I circulated throughout the room, making notes of the types of comments I heard on an index card.

These quick anecdotal notes showed me the type of thinking each student was doing. When I have a particular student I'm worried about, I listen more carefully to that student's comments. Sometimes I'll even use a tape recorder to capture the entire conversation. Then, I go back and look at the comments to figure out what type of skill is revealed through the comment. To help you do this, you'll find a Listening to Student Talk card in the front pocket of this binder. Use this card to record student comments as you circulate throughout the room.

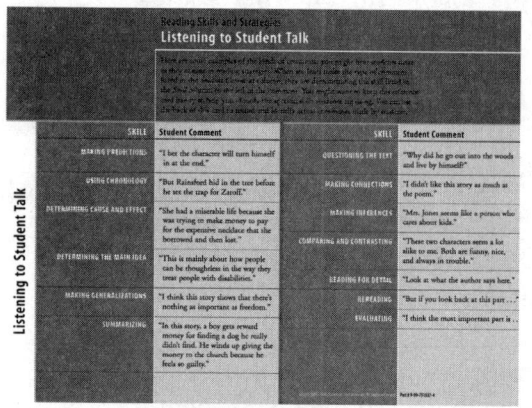

Occasionally, I'll take student comments and transfer them to a transparency that I then show to the entire class. I'll show students the types of comments I heard while circulating around the room, and then we'll discuss the types of thinking their comments reveal.

While this debriefing isn't mandatory for students, it is mandatory for you, the teacher. If you aren't listening to your students' comments, then you aren't hearing evidence of the thinking that strategies encourage. If you don't hear evidence of their thinking, then you really don't know if the strategy is effective or not—especially the strategies that don't result in a written product. So, as students use the strategies, try to capture their comments on paper and then look at those comments to see what insights they offer you into your students' thinking. That glimpse into their thinking processes will give you valuable information that can point the way to the direction you need to take your teaching next.

In addition to assessing students' thinking, some of the strategies result in specific written products. That leads to the second type of assessment you should consider. Strategies like Somebody Wanted But So, Text Reformulation, Story Impressions, and Save the Last Word for Me result in written products. Thus, in addition to assessing students' thinking with these strategies, you can also assess their written products, much as you would any piece of writing they create.

Finally, you need to let students participate in self-assessment. To help students see how strategies are benefiting them, I occasionally ask them to complete a brief survey like the one below. Often, I will let them keep these surveys so that, over time, they can see evidence of their progress and note how their use of a specific strategy has changed.

Name _____ Date _____ Strategy _____

Complete each statement:

1. I like this strategy because . . .
   ....
   ....

2. I dislike this strategy because . . .
   ....
   ....

3. This strategy helps me . . .
   ....
   ....

I often add specific questions for specific strategies. For instance, if students have been using the Think-Aloud strategy (page 115), I'll ask them to look at their tally sheets, determine what type of comments they make most frequently and least frequently, and reflect on *why* they think they make or don't make certain kinds of comments. If students have completed Most Important Word (page 35), I might ask them to look back over the last several Most Important Word strategies they've done and notice from which portion of a text they tend to choose the Most Important Word. If students can see that they always choose a word from the beginning of a story as opposed to the climax, that might indicate a lack of awareness of rising action. It might also mean that the student is drawn to exciting beginnings. And, of course, it could simply indicate that the student predicts well. What's interesting is to see what the *student* thinks it means.

For almost every strategy, there is something specific you can do to add to the general assessment. Again, the point is to help students see that reading involves thinking and that strategies encourage them to engage in the kind of thinking they need to be doing.

Side Trip #4: Using Strategies to Overcome Aliteracy

I think we encounter *aliterate* students—more commonly called reluctant readers—at least as often and perhaps more often than struggling readers. Reluctant readers dislike the entire process of reading, even though they might actually read well. For those of us who like to read, understanding why someone who *could* read wouldn't *want* to read is a mystery. To help solve that mystery, and to understand how strategies might help these students, let's first look at what reluctant readers say about reading.

About eight years after Ben (remember Ben?), I had a student named Kendra. Unlike Ben, who was truly a struggling reader, Kendra could read; she just hated it. Here's what Kendra had to say about reading:

Kendra: It's like, like so boring, you know?
KB: Boring because . . . ?
Kendra: I don't know. You know it's just like boring sitting there looking at those words.
KB: But don't those words sometimes tell a good story?
Kendra: Words tell a story? *[pause]* I don't think so. I mean, it's like it's just words, you know?

Kendra offered me valuable insight into the various ways that different types of reluctant readers perceived reading. Some of them, like Kendra, say only that it's "boring," or "just words." What they are not able to say is that they are bored because they don't know how to visualize the text.

How can you motivate students who consider reading to be "calling words" or "saying words" or "just words on page"? They find it almost impossible to create either images or personal connections as they read. When you ask them what would motivate them to read, they are likely to first answer "nothing." In reality, though, if you watch them closely, you will see some things that *do* motivate them. Because they don't form a lot of images when they read, they prefer books with illustrations. In addition, struggling and reluctant readers prefer nonfiction over the fiction that abounds in the literature classroom. Also, because reluctant readers don't know authors, don't know genre, and see a library as "too big," they really don't know "where any of the good books are." They need our help in choosing books.

Reluctant readers also benefit enormously from hearing books read aloud. That has less to do with being lazy and more to do with desiring a dramatic interpretation of the book as an aid to visualizing. Similarly, reluctant readers like viewing the movie before reading the book—again, the movie acts as a scaffold to provide a visual image. Finally, these students enjoy art activities based on books—anything that helps them make those words on a page something they can *see*.

For skilled readers, one strong motivation for reading is the appeal of belonging to a community of readers. While reading may begin as a solitary act, it quickly becomes a way to interact with a group, to take part in discussions, to swap favorite stories, and to argue over themes. Reading becomes, as Bloome (1987) explains, "a social process—a means to participate in and establish a community or social group."

Reluctant readers, on the other hand, aren't particularly interested in activities that cause them to connect with other readers. Many times this is because they doubt they have anything of value to say to another reader. In the words of one student, "Sometimes [it's] really embarrassing because it's like I don't have anything to say." Continually facing embarrassment, these students eventually convince themselves that they were right to not like reading in the first place. To help these reluctant readers move into a community of readers, use strategies that not only provide them with the opportunity to enter into discussions but also give them direction on what to say. For instance, the Say Something strategy (page 65) offers students an opportunity to pause throughout the text to make specific kinds of comments: predictions, connections, questions, or comments. That tiny bit of scaffolding not only makes the strategy accessible, but also turns the activity into something inherently more motivating.

So, the answer to the question, *Will the strategies help me with my reluctant readers?* is Yes. Some of the strategies will enhance the types of activities these students find motivational. Other strategies will encourage them to become part of the community of readers.

This Handbook as Your Guidebook

This *Reading Skills and Strategies: Reaching Struggling Readers* binder is divided into two parts: the *Reading Strategies Handbook* that you're reading now and the *MiniRead Skills Lessons and Selection Skills Lessons* (all those other pages!). This *Reading Strategies Handbook* explains each of the strategies shown in the chart on pages 5–6. I hope you'll read about these strategies—some of which may already be familiar to you—and use them with a variety of texts, helping your students to build an "arsenal" of strategies that they can apply to any reading situation.

To help you apply the strategies to the selections in the *Elements of Literature* anthology, we've provided Teaching Notes, blackline masters, and transparencies (the contents of the rest of this binder) that show you how to use a strategy with a particular selection in order to help students with a specific reading skill. The reading skills—everything from Monitoring Comprehension to Making Generalizations—appear with the Pupil's Edition selections on the Before You Read pages, under the heading "Reading Skills and Strategies."

In addition to the Selection Skills Lessons, you'll find something called MiniReads, with their accompanying MiniRead Skills Lessons. When I started working on this project, I was adamant that struggling and reluctant readers have the opportunity to first practice the strategies on easy-to-read texts. I thought that expecting struggling readers to learn a new strategy while working through a piece of literature would be too much to ask. Thus, I developed MiniReads—short, easy-to-read texts (both fiction and nonfiction) that serve as easier, more motivating selections in which to practice each strategy before applying it to a literary work in the anthology. Although each MiniRead accompanies a particular strategy, you can, if you wish, reuse MiniReads with different strategies. So, when you want to spend extra time practicing a certain strategy but have already used the MiniRead we've connected to that strategy, just turn to other MiniReads in the binder and choose one of those.

Final Words

Ben started me thinking about what I didn't know. Al showed me a major flaw in how I was trying to teach. Belinda, Eric, Kendra, and countless other students along the way have accompanied me, guided me, and inspired me on my journey of learning and teaching. This *Reading Skills and Strategies Handbook* is filled with student voices and based on classroom situations I've encountered. I've changed students' and teachers' names and sometimes altered grade levels to protect identities, but I haven't changed their actual words, for it is through the words of our students that we can move toward an understanding of why they struggle with reading and learn how strategies can ease such struggles.

It's a difficult time in which we teach. That you return year after year to the classroom in spite of the difficulties speaks highly of you. It's also a difficult time in which to be a student. That struggling readers return year after year to classrooms where they daily look failure in the eye speaks highly of them. Some students don't return; they finally give up and drop out. I feel my biggest sense of failure with those students. Other students return, but in body only; they've built a wall around themselves, and apathy has become their middle name. But some struggling students return with a sense of willingness, hopeful that this is the year they'll finally "get it," that this is the year they'll stop struggling. Hearing past their snide remarks and seeing past their blasé looks is sometimes a challenge. But adolescents who show up daily in classes are telling us with their presence that they are willing to learn. You may become, for many of these students, their best chance for success. If that's true, then you need every tool possible to help these students. Strategies that facilitate reading skills are powerful tools. Struggling readers deserve no less.

References

Beers, Kylene. 1996a. No Time, No Interest, No Way! Part I. *School Library Journal* 42(2): 30–33.

Beers, Kylene. 1996b. No Time, No Interest, No Way! Part II. *School Library Journal* 42(3):110–113.

Bloome, David. 1987. *Literacy and Schooling.* Norwood, NJ: Ablex Publishing.

Olshavsky, Jill Edwards. 1976–77. Reading as Problem-Solving: An Investigation of Strategies. *Reading Research Quarterly* 12: 654–674.

Paris, Scott G., Barbara A. Wasik, and J. C. Turner. 1991. The Development of Strategic Readers. In *Handbook of Reading Research: Volume II,* edited by Rebecca Barr, Michael L. Kamil, Peter B. Mosenthal, and P. D. Pearson. New York: Longman.

Routman, Regie. 1992. Teach Skills with a Strategy. *Instructor* 101(9): 34–37.

Tierney, Robert J., John E. Readence, and Ernest K. Dishner. 1995. *Reading Strategies and Practices: A Compendium.* 4th edition. Boston, MA: Allyn & Bacon.

Wallis, John. 1998. Strategies: What Connects Readers to Meaning. In *Into Focus: Understanding and Creating Middle School Readers,* edited by Kylene Beers and Barbara Samuels. Norwood, MA: Christopher-Gordon Publishers.

ANTICIPATION GUIDES STRATEGY

Little kids do it. They constantly ask what's going on and where they are being taken. Big kids do it. They ask what the doctor is going to do before the doctor does it, and they plan what they'll say when they are approaching parents with special requests. Adults do it. We pick up travel brochures before we travel, study maps before we make a car trip, and check out the checkbook before we make a purchase. We all do it—we try to anticipate what's going to happen before it actually happens.

Good readers consciously try to anticipate what a text is about before they begin reading. They look at the cover, art, title, genre, author, headings, graphs, charts, length, print size, inside flaps, and back cover. I've even seen students reading the bibliographic information on the copyright page. They ask friends, "Is this any good?" They do anything to find out something about a text before they begin reading.

Struggling readers, on the other hand, often don't do that; they are told to read something, and once the text is in hand, they just begin. They often skip titles and background information, hardly ever read book jackets, and rarely look through the text for clues. The assignment is to read, so they'll read—maybe. We know they'd read better, however, if they brought to reading what they bring to the rest of life: anticipation.

To help students learn to anticipate, use **Anticipation Guides** (Tierney, Readence, and Dishner 1995). An Anticipation Guide is a set of generaliza-

ANTICIPATION GUIDES STRATEGY

tions related to the theme of a selection. Students decide whether they agree or disagree with each statement in the guide. These guides activate students' prior knowledge, encourage them to make personal connections to what they will be reading, and give them clues to what the text is about.

Step into a Classroom

A Classroom Model

"This is hard," one student from the back row complained as he looked up from the paper he was working on.

"Yeah," another said.

The teacher just smiled and nodded. "Hmm," he responded.

"Aw, come on, Mr. Davidson. These questions are really hard," the student said again.

Another student in the middle of the room looked up and said, "Not really hard like 'What's the answer?' but hard like it's tough to make a choice."

"Hmm," Mr. Davidson said again, smiling.

The students kept reading and completing the worksheet. Occasionally they looked up and said things like "Impossible" or "This is tough" or "Well, it depends," but kept working.

As they finished, Mr. Davidson finally spoke: "Do you want to talk about the statements now or later?"

"Now," eighteen voices replied.

"Okay. Let's just get a count of how many agreed and how many disagreed, and then we'll come back and discuss. How many of you agreed with number 1: 'If you are going to be a good citizen, then you should always do what your government expects'?" Some hands went up; others stayed down.

"It's that word *always*, Mr. Davidson. What if bad people start running the government?" a student said.

Mr. Davidson said "Hmm." They all laughed. Then the teacher started a chart of agree/disagree responses on the board. "Number 2: 'Hiding people that the government says are criminals is wrong.'" More hands up, still some hands down. "All right. Number 3: 'If you have limited food and limited space and are trying hard to make sure your family survives, you shouldn't be expected to take in other people who will make your supplies disappear even faster.'"

Before hands could go up, a student spoke up. "That one was really hard, Mr. Davidson. I mean, you know that you should take in people that need help, but if you are trying to help your own family to survive, then you could like really hurt them if you say yes. But if you say no, then you are one cold dude."

ANTICIPATION GUIDES STRATEGY

"Yeah," came a chorus of supporters.

"Hmm," Mr. Davidson said.

"Aw, come on," several said, smiling.

"Aren't you going to help us at all?" one asked.

"No," Mr. Davidson said, shaking his head.

"So we just have to decide?" another asked.

"Yes," Mr. Davidson said. "Now, how many agree?" Hands went up. "Number 4," he said after counting, "says, 'People who do cruel things can still be good people.'" More moans, but students finally raised hands showing if they agreed or disagreed.

After getting a sense of what the class thought about each statement, Mr. Davidson returned to each point and began a discussion. Several students made comments about the last item, "People who do cruel things can still be good people."

Mr. Davidson:	So, what do you think?
Albert:	I think that's wrong. How could you be good and cruel at the same time?
Kii:	Well, what if you didn't want to be cruel but had to do a bad thing to survive? Like my uncle when he was leaving Vietnam. He had to steal some things because the government wasn't letting any more people out, and they weren't even supposed to leave. My cousin got into a fight and hurt another guy real bad, he thinks, but my cousin had to or the guy would have told what they were doing. My cousin and my uncle are not bad people.
Isaac:	Well, maybe sometimes you got to do what you do. But when people are just doin' stuff, that's wrong.
Dee:	I think sometimes if you're bad, you're bad. That's it. But sometimes you're bad 'cause that's the way the world makes you. You're tryin' to do right, but you have to join with a crew just to survive. Bein' in a crew, sometimes you do cold stuff.
Isaac:	Yeah, you do what you got to do.
Mr. Davidson:	Okay, interesting thoughts, guys. Do you think you are the first group to ever have to face making choices about what you will do or won't do? Do you think you are the first group to wonder how far you'll go to protect yourself or those you love? It's happened throughout time to all sorts of people. One group of people has often tried to control another group. Now we are going to read a play about one girl's attempt to survive against a group that doesn't want her to survive. As you read the play, find the parts that address the issues we've been talking about. Go ahead and jot down page numbers on your Anticipation Guide. You'll find parts of the play

ANTICIPATION GUIDES STRATEGY

that make you think more about each of the statements we just discussed. After you have finished reading, look at those parts again and think about your responses. If something you've read has changed whether or not you agree with the statement, make a note of it and then we'll talk about what you are thinking. Now this play is going to take several days to read. . . .

What's Going On?

These students were working through an Anticipation Guide for *The Diary of Anne Frank*. Mr. Davidson had purposely created statements that were "tough" to answer, as one student pointed out. The goal of the discussion wasn't to change students' minds but to bring issues to their awareness.

Anticipation Guides first act as a prereading strategy and encourage students to think about issues and make predictions. Then, they allow students to look for cause-and-effect relationships as they read. Finally, they allow students to generalize, to discuss those generalizations, and to explore their own responses to a text.

Through the Anticipation Guide, these students explored their own thoughts about issues they would encounter in the play. They were anticipating what they might find and were ready to make those discoveries.

Getting the Strategy to Work

- **First, write the Anticipation Guide.** If you read the text and look for the big ideas or themes that are presented, you'll have a start on what will make good items to include in the guide. If one of the issues in the text is survival, jot down generalizations about survival, keeping the most debatable, thought-provoking ones. You don't need a lot of items; two items that encourage discussion are better than ten items that inspire little debate. Students should mark each statement as one with which they agree or disagree rather than as true or false. You want them to explore what they believe about the statement. Make sure your statements don't have a right or wrong answer; otherwise, the guide will be ineffective. Suppose a history teacher used this Anticipation Guide to introduce a unit on the Holocaust:

    1. It is wrong to persecute people because of their religious beliefs.

    2. Hitler should not have ordered the extermination of the Jews.

    3. Keeping a diary is a good way to record your feelings.

    4. We should study the Holocaust to understand our past mistakes.

ANTICIPATION GUIDES STRATEGY

Every student would simply mark "agree" for each item, since each statement has an obvious conclusion. The guide would not be meaningful to students because it would not build anticipation. Effective Anticipation Guides present students with pertinent issues that are worth discussing but that don't have clear-cut answers.

Effective Anticipation Guides present students with pertinent issues that are worth discussing but that don't have clear-cut answers.

- **Introduce the strategy to students.** The best way to teach students how to use an Anticipation Guide is simply to do one with them. Make sure students understand that they aren't guessing the correct answer but are exploring their thoughts. You might write an Anticipation Guide for the fairy tale "Cinderella," including statements such as the following:

1. Sometimes life hands you cruel situations; when that happens, the best thing to do is just to get through the situation. You'll eventually get a reward.	Agree Disagree
2. You should always be willing to turn the other cheek; in other words, if someone treats you poorly, you shouldn't fight back but should just keep on doing what you know is right.	Agree Disagree

These two brief statements elicit a discussion that encourages students to anticipate what they will read, to find how these statements play themselves out in the text, and to return to the statements after reading, ready to have some meaningful discussions.

- **Use Anticipation Guides before, during, and after reading.** Before reading, students should complete an Anticipation Guide that addresses issues in the selection. After students have completed the Anticipation Guide and you've talked about their responses, tell students to keep the guide handy as they read, so they can make notes about issues as they are revealed in the text. After students have finished reading, have them look at their original responses to see if their opinions have changed. The reading may have changed their responses by strengthening their original positions or by making them doubt those positions.

ANTICIPATION GUIDES STRATEGY

A Few Questions . . .

1. **Can an Anticipation Guide be used as a pretest and posttest?**
   I've seen teachers use it in that way, but I don't find that to be very effective. It is more effective to use it either as a before-, during-, and after-reading strategy or as a brainstorming activity for writing.

2. **Can Anticipation Guides be used for a topic or issue that students don't know anything about?**
   That's exactly when you need to use them. A major reason for using an Anticipation Guide is to activate students' prior knowledge. If students are about to read something that is outside of their experience (say, reading Shakespeare for the first time), then we must build some bridges between their experiences and the text; otherwise, the reading will be for naught. That's why Anticipation Guides aren't based on facts but on generalizations you can draw from the text.

3. **Should the class always discuss their responses to the Anticipation Guide before reading the text?**
   Not necessarily. I've told students to respond to the guide; read the text, taking notes about parts that relate to issues in the guide; and then return to the guide to mark whether or not they still agree. At other times, I've simply had students discuss their responses, as Mr. Davidson did. Do what works for that particular selection or class.

References

Tierney, Robert J., John E. Readence, and Ernest K. Dishner. 1995. *Reading Strategies and Practices: A Compendium.* 4th ed. Needham Heights, Mass.: Allyn & Bacon.

ANTICIPATION GUIDES STRATEGY

Anticipation Guides at a Glance

- The teacher writes the Anticipation Guide, a set of generalizations based on issues in the text and designed to promote discussion and predictions about the text.

- Students mark whether they agree or disagree with each statement, then discuss their responses.

- While students read, they take notes on the issues in the guide as those issues are revealed in the text.

- After reading, students look at their responses again to see whether they still agree or disagree with each statement.

IT SAYS...I SAY STRATEGY

Please read the following: The bridnic scroffelled the ibnic. The ibnic scroffelled the flibberrond. The flibberrond scroffelled the webernet. Now answer the following questions:

1. What did the bridnic scroffell?
2. Did the ibnic scroffell the flibberrond or the bridnic?
3. What scroffelled the webernet?

Here are the answers:

1. The bridnic scroffelled the ibnic.
2. The ibnic scroffelled the flibberrond.
3. The flibberrond scroffelled the webernet.

Did you answer all the questions correctly? Probably you did, because to answer those questions, you didn't have to understand what a *bridnic* or an *ibnic*, or even a *flibberrond*, is. You just needed to match words in the questions to words in the text. But look at the next question:

4. Would you rather be a bridnic, an ibnic, or a flibberrond?

Hmm. Now there's a problem. You can't answer this one until you know what *bridnic*, *ibnic*, and *flibberrond* mean. And it would probably help a lot to know what *scroffelled* means. Then, you could combine what you know about each of those words with what happens to each of those words in the text and draw your own conclusion about which you'd prefer to be. That type of thinking—combining something from the text with something you already

IT SAYS...I SAY STRATEGY

know—is called inferential thinking. Skilled readers make inferences as they read; struggling readers often don't. The inability to make inferences creates problems for readers that often result in statements like "I don't get it" and "How'd you know that?" To help students understand how inferences are formed, use a strategy called **It Says . . . I Say**. Completing an It Says . . . I Say chart helps students visualize and internalize the steps of making an inference—combining the information in the text with the information they already know.

Step into a Classroom

A Classroom Model

"When you finish reading," Mr. Arlin said, "answer the questions at the end of the story. If you need to, use the It Says . . . I Say chart."

"Tell me again when we need to use it," a girl in the fourth row said.

"Okay, everybody, look this way," Mr. Arlin said, walking to the large chart that hung on the wall.

It Says...I Say...And So

Question	It Says	I Say	And So
1. Read the question.	2. Find information from the text that will help you answer the question.	3. Think about what you know about that information.	4. Combine what the text says with what you know to make an inference and answer the question.

"Remember, people, we've been using this chart to help us answer certain questions. Anybody remember what kind of questions?" Mr. Arlin asked.

Silence. This was a class of sixteen students, all fourteen or fifteen years old, all of whom read at about a fourth-grade level. All were in the class because they had repeatedly failed the reading portion of the state achievement test.

IT SAYS... I SAY STRATEGY

"I'll ask again: What kind of questions does the chart help you answer?"

A boy in the first row answered, "Uh, you know, those inferred questions."

"Good job, Isaac," Mr. Arlin said. "Now, who can tell us what inferential questions are?"

A tall young man said, "Questions where we have to use the chart." Everyone laughed, including Mr. Arlin.

"Sorry, Benjamin. You'll have to do better than that," Mr. Arlin responded.

"Oh, you know, like those kinds of questions where the answer isn't there in the book, so you gotta think about it, and you gotta already know somethin' about it," Benjamin said.

"That's it," Mr. Arlin said. "Now, some of the questions at the end of this story won't have the answer in the story. That doesn't mean that the story is dumb, that the questions can't be answered, or that you are stupid; it means you've got to think about the question differently. You must take what's in the story, combine that with what you know, and then come up with your answer."

It Says... I Say... And So

Question	It Says	I Say	And So
Why did Goldilocks break Baby Bear's chair?	Story says she sits down in the baby chair but she's no baby.	Baby chairs aren't very big because they're for babies, and she is bigger, so she weighs more.	And so she is too heavy for it and it breaks.

"Mr. Arlin, I don't get it," a girl in the second row said.

"She wasn't here when we did it," another girl interjected.

"Okay, who remembers Goldilocks?" Mr. Arlin asked.

"I do," another boy said. "Goldilocks went into the three bears' house, and

IT SAYS... I SAY STRATEGY

she ate their porridge and sat in their chairs and broke the baby's chair and went to sleep in the baby's bed. So why did she break Baby Bear's chair?"

"Because it was a baby chair, so it was little and she was big, so she was too heavy and it broke," a boy called out.

"Marcus," Mr. Arlin said to the boy who offered that answer, "come up to the board, and using the It Says . . . I Say chart, show us how you came up with your answer."

Marcus walked to the board and wrote his answer in the chart (see the It Says . . . I Say chart on page 27).

"Okay, people," Mr. Arlin said. "Look up here, because this is correct. Marcus wrote down the question and the information from the story. But remember, the story doesn't tell you that Goldilocks is too big for the chair, so Marcus had to think about how kids are bigger than babies, how they weigh more, and how they can break baby furniture because it isn't strong enough to hold heavy people. Then he made his inference and answered the question. Goldilocks breaks the chair because she is too heavy for it."

"Cool," the girl who had been absent remarked.

"Okay. Are we ready to read?" No noise. "Finish reading, then answer the questions. Students who use the chart correctly will get a special congratulatory handshake from me."

Laughter and moans erupted as students opened their books and settled down to read.

The next day, students came back to class with most of the questions answered. As they discussed their answers to the questions that required an inference, students shared their charts. Here's how one student modeled her answer for another student:

Faith: What'd you say?
Karen: Well, I thought it was hard. But I made my chart like this [*she lays down her paper; see chart on page* 29]:
Faith: I got that about the money coming from bad ways, but I didn't put that part about not wanting to do wrong.
Karen: That just seemed important, or why not take the money even though you know it's stolen?
Faith: Yeah, that's what helps you know he is not going to take it. Okay, that's why I couldn't see if he should have taken it or not, since they needed the money and all, but you're right about how he never wanted to do wrong. Then you know that he was right. That's good.

After observing students use the It Says . . . I Say strategy, I asked Mr. Arlin why on the first day he still had Marcus write his answer on the board using the chart's structure, even though he had given the right answer.

IT SAYS... I SAY STRATEGY

It Says... I Say... And So

Question	It Says	I Say	And So
Was Johnson right to refuse the money?	The story says that he was "sure the money had come to Peterson from bad ways."	I think that "bad ways" must mean that Peterson got the money illegally.	And so I think he was right to refuse the money.
	It says that Johnson "always knew right from wrong and never wanted to be the one doing wrong."	I think that since Johnson doesn't want to do wrong, then he would feel bad if he took the money.	

"Marcus is a bright young man. I don't know if he answered the question about why the chair broke because he remembered that example from a few days ago, because he made the inference on his own, or because he understood how to use It Says... I Say as a way to get to the answer. What I do know is that I've got students in my class who don't understand how to make inferences. They needed to see how Marcus got to that answer. By having him put the answer on the board, following the chart's structure, those students were able to see how an inference is created."

"So some of your students think that the answers to inferential questions are supposed to be in the text?" I asked.

"I'm not really sure," he said. "But I do know that once questions move beyond the literal level, the students flounder. With this strategy, though, they see how to think."

"Once questions move beyond the literal level, the students flounder. With this strategy, though, they see how to think."

IT SAYS...I SAY STRATEGY

What's Going On?

Seeing how to think. I liked Mr. Arlin's phrase, and I believe it is an accurate description of what the It Says...I Say chart does for students. Mr. Arlin's students, like many struggling readers, generally responded to inference questions with comments like "How am I supposed to answer this? The answer isn't here," or "This is a dumb question," or even "I'm too stupid to answer this question." These students spend so much effort just getting through the text, just keeping up with the literal details—characters, events, setting—that making an inference as they read is the last thing that happens, if it happens at all. Therefore, when they encounter a question that requires an inference, they don't know where to begin. They need a strategy that helps them internalize the process of how to infer.

> *The It Says . . . I Say chart helps students finally see a structure for making an inference.*

Getting the Strategy to Work

Repeated practice is the key to success when using It Says...I Say. In the previous classroom example, Mr. Arlin had to go over the strategy with students again, even though he had obviously talked with them before about how to use it. He also had hung the It Says...I Say chart in the classroom so that students could refer to it.

- **Introduce the strategy to students using a short, familiar story** (such as "The Three Bears" or "The Three Little Pigs" or a story students are currently reading). Ask a few literal-level questions, questions that Taffy Raphael calls Right There Questions (Raphael 1982). Then, ask a question that requires students to make an inference. If a student answers it correctly, ask that student to explain how the inference was created using the It Says...I Say chart that you'll have already made (see the chart on page 26). Have the student write what the text says about the question in the *It Says* column, what he or she already knows about the question in the *I Say* column, and the inference formed by combining these two columns in the *And So* column. If no one can answer the question, answer it yourself, writing your responses on the chart.

- **Model the strategy regularly.** As with everything we teach, modeling is the key. Remember that struggling readers often need multiple models over an extended period of time. But you don't always have to be the model. In Mr. Arlin's classroom, Marcus did the modeling. The next day, Karen and Faith shared their answers to inference questions. That sharing became another form of modeling. As Faith saw how Karen worked through the answer, she came to understand not only how Karen reached her conclusion, but also why she herself couldn't "see" the answer.

IT SAYS... I SAY STRATEGY

Struggling readers often say things about not being able to visualize what is happening in the text—and that might include not being able to visualize the connections between what is happening in the text and what is already in their minds. Those connections are what form inferences. The It Says . . . I Say chart is the visual form of those connections. Eventually, you want students to make inferences in their heads; until then, they may need the extra support of this strategy. The chart will enable you to see students' thinking, and students will be able to see the connections they need to form.

> *Struggling readers often say things about not being able to visualize what is happening in the text.*

A Few Questions . . .

1. Is it important to quote from the text?
Students can either quote from the text or paraphrase the text. Since the *It Says* column refers directly to the text, the more direct quotations students use, the better. In her chart, Karen writes a comment in the *I Say* column for each quotation from the text. That's important. Then she reached one conclusion.

2. Doesn't this chart get lengthy?
Yes. That means you need to look ahead at the questions you want students to answer. If there are six questions and all six require an inference, that's probably too much writing for struggling readers. If that's the case, consider having students work in pairs or small groups to answer some questions. Also, remember that as soon as you see that students can make inferences and tell you how they have reached those inferences, then they don't need to complete the chart repeatedly. The chart is a scaffold to be used as needed.

3. Where can I find inferential questions to use with students?
You'll find a variety of questions that require inferences in the "Making Meanings" sections that accompany selections in *Elements of Literature*. These questions provide students with lots of opportunities to use the chart to practice making inferences.

IT SAYS... I SAY STRATEGY

4. **How do you make sure students get all the important information on the *It Says* part of the chart before they go on to the rest of the chart?**

    Good question. Some students might need more support than just the chart; they might need to be told how many items to list under the *It Says* column. So you might need to look ahead at the questions; think about the answers; and tell students that for a certain question, they should find one, two, or three items from the text for their *It Says* column. Eventually, you want students to decide this for themselves; but in the beginning, you might have to provide that support.

5. **How can I tell whether a student can't make an inference or just got the wrong answer?**

    I find that students who can't make inferences often skip inferential questions entirely. These students need the chart to help them answer the question. Students who can make inferences but simply have made wrong inferences also benefit from using the chart.

6. **So what can I expect when students use the It Says... I Say strategy?**

    Many readers have a difficult time just "getting through" a text. They don't know how to identify significant details in a text and combine them with their own knowledge to form inferences. By using the It Says... I Say chart, students break down the steps of making an inference and see what kinds of thinking they need to do. Eventually students will internalize the inferencing process and will be able to make inferences without the help of the chart.

References

Raphael, Taffy. 1982. Question-Answering Strategies for Children. *The Reading Teacher* 36:186–190.

IT SAYS...I SAY STRATEGY

It Says...I Say at a Glance

- The teacher creates a model It Says...I Say chart for the classroom. The chart consists of four columns in which students write a question that requires an inference, what the text says about the question (*It Says*), what they already know about that information (*I Say*), and their inference (*And So*).

- The teacher models the strategy using an inferential question based on a familiar story.

- Students practice making inferences by using the chart regularly to explain their answers to inferential questions.

MOST IMPORTANT WORD STRATEGY

After four years of teaching seventh-grade language arts I thought I understood how to create a response-centered classroom, but something just wasn't happening. Students listened to each other's responses to the text and agreed or disagreed, but whenever I asked, "What message are you carrying away from this story?" the conversation stopped.

One day I finally began to understand what was going on. During a discussion of O. Henry's "The Gift of the Magi," I asked, "What was the message that you got from this story?" Thirty-three sets of eyes immediately traveled quickly to their books. Students began turning pages and looking up and down the columns of text. "Wait a minute," I said after a moment had passed. They looked up. "Why are you all looking at your books?" No one said anything.

Finally, one student said, "Personally, I'm praying that someone wrote in the margin what the message is." We all laughed.

"But why don't you just ask yourself what the message is? I'm not asking you what message you think the author might have been presenting. I'm asking you what you got from it." Again, everyone sat for a long pause.

Then the same student said, "Well, that's like really hard. I mean, *message*. What message? That's just such a big question."

For many students, the question is too broad, too open. One strategy that students can use to help them answer the question is **Most Important Word** (Bleich 1975). Most Important Word is a postreading strategy in which stu-

MOST IMPORTANT WORD STRATEGY

dents decide which word in a text they think is the most important based on specific evidence in the text. As students decide which word is the most important, they begin to formulate their responses to the question "What did the story mean to you?" Having students look for the most important word not only leads to meaningful discussions about the message of the text, but also improves the students' abilities to summarize, recognize cause-and-effect relationships, identify main ideas, and make inferences and generalizations.

Step into a Classroom

A Classroom Model

Six students had pulled their desks into a close circle. All of them had copies of Caroline Cooney's *Driver's Ed* on their desks. One of the students began speaking.

Karen: Okay, we'll go first. Leslie and I chose *sign* as the most important word. We thought it was most important because that is mainly what this story is about—the way the kids take that sign and then what it did. If Remy and Morgan hadn't taken the sign, then Denise wouldn't have died, so that is what starts everything happening. And it is mentioned on almost every page.

Benjamin: Yeah, we thought about *sign*, but me and Lee said *love* was the most important word. We agree that taking the sign was what got everything started, but then everyone was so angry at them that they didn't think anyone loved them anymore. Like Morgan's mother—she was so cold. At least Remy's mother finally said she still loved them, but Morgan's mother—well, she was so worried about her perfect family that she was just cold.

Lee: But if everyone had just patted the kids on the head and said it was okay and kept on loving them, then there wouldn't have been any book. What kept the book going was them wondering how to go on if no one in their families loved them anymore. It was like the motivation for the book. [*pause*]

Maria: Are you done? [*Benjamin and Lee nod.*] Okay. Amelia and me decided on *mercy*.

Benjamin: Mercy? Where is that used?

Amelia: It's on pages 114 and 115. [*Most of the students turn to those pages.*] See? His dad is talking about mercy, and then at the top

MOST IMPORTANT WORD STRATEGY

	of page 115, Morgan wonders how much mercy he gets. Mercy is sort of like forgiveness, but it seemed like even more.
Maria:	Right. It's like forgiveness is saying, "We know you didn't mean to and we forgive you," but mercy is what you need to be able to do the forgiveness. Without mercy there's no forgiveness.
Karen:	It doesn't say that.
Maria:	No, that's just what we thought.
Benjamin:	Yeah, but how can *mercy* be the most important word when it isn't used but on these two pages?
Maria:	It isn't about how often a word is used, but what is the most important.
Leslie:	I still say that *sign* is important. And it isn't just the sign that the kids took, but Morgan keeps looking for a sign. Look at page 114, where you found *mercy*. It says, "Give me a way out, Morgan thought. A sign that I don't have to worry about the sign."
Amelia:	Oh, that's cool. Like a message. And like the stop sign.
Leslie:	I don't know. Yeah, maybe. But the important word is *sign*. All through the book people are looking for signs. Remy is looking for a sign that Morgan likes her. Then they are looking for real signs like street signs. Then there's no stop sign, so Denise doesn't know to be looking for it. Then Morgan looks for some sort of sign that his mother still loves him. And both Remy and Morgan are looking for a sign that they will be forgiven.
Karen:	And then remember the part when the baby plays with Remy's necklace? Later Remy says she will wear it every day to remind her of Denise. So then the necklace becomes like a sign.
Benjamin:	Yeah, I agree that *sign* is important, but after they take the stop sign, what kind of sign are they looking for the rest of the time? A sign that they are still loved. I still think that *sign* is what gets everything going, but then them worrying about whether their parents still love them is what the rest of the book is about.

These students continued to discuss the most important word for another fifteen minutes. Amelia soon gave up her position that *mercy* was the most important word, and instead agreed that the most important word was *sign*. Afterward, the students put their desks back in order and each began working on an essay that explained his or her choice of the most important word. Students were directed to end their essays by explaining how the most important word related to the message they found in the book. Benjamin's essay shows that he supports his assertions with the text and uses important reading skills:

MOST IMPORTANT WORD STRATEGY

    I think that <u>love</u> is the most important word in the book <u>Driver's Ed</u>. Remy and Morgan steal a stop sign and a lady named Denise drives through that intersection and is killed because she didn't stop and a truck broadsided her car. Then, Remy and Morgan feel guilty. They want their parents to forgive them and they want Denise's husband to forgive them. Then, they realize that they can never really be forgiven because what they did was really terrible. So, what they want is just for their parents to love them even with what they did. Remy finally gets so desperate for love that she says to her mother, "I don't care how mad you are at me. I'm very mad at me, too. But you have to go on loving me." Then her mother tells her that she does still love her, but she is still angry with her. Morgan tells his dad, "I don't think I deserve love." His dad tells him, "Nobody deserves it. Love just is." So finally, Remy and Morgan understand that their parents still love them even though they did a terrible thing, and their parents realize that, too.

    That's the message I got from this book—that sometimes what starts out as a stupid prank can really hurt people. When that happens, people have a right to get angry but in the middle of all that anger, you can still love people and that's the only thing that will ever make some tragedies better. This was a really good book.

inference

generalization

MOST IMPORTANT WORD STRATEGY

What's Going On?

Having students find the most important word offers them opportunities to make inferences and generalizations, summarize, sequence, discuss the main idea, and think about cause-and-effect relationships. In the previous discussion, Maria makes a generalization when she explains the difference between mercy and forgiveness. Leslie, when she lists the references to signs in the novel, is sequencing events. When Karen explains her choice of the word *sign*, she identifies a main idea and recognizes cause-and-effect relationships.

Many times when you ask students to find the main idea or to make a generalization or discuss the message, they don't do it. They sit, they stare, they look through the pages of their books, but they don't offer many answers. Most Important Word leads to revealing discussions that cause students to use those skills as they read and reflect on what they have read.

> *Most Important Word leads to revealing discussions that cause students to . . . reflect on what they have read.*

Getting the Strategy to Work

- **Introduce the strategy.** Like all the other strategies, modeling this strategy is important. Model it by reading a short text, such as a picture book or a poem, and then by talking through how you decided which word was the most important. Make sure that you refer to specific evidence in the text to support your opinions.

- **Discuss the selection.** Give students time to discuss the story before you ask them what the most important word is. Let them respond to parts of the text that they liked or didn't like, that they didn't understand, or that remind them of something else.

- **Allow adequate time for students to make their choices.** Give students time to really think about what the most important word is. One teacher using this strategy with her students had them read and discuss a story; then she said, "Okay, I'm going to give you a minute or two to think of the most important word in the story." After about two minutes, she called time and asked students what the most important word was. She was surprised when most students either said nothing or just agreed with what someone else said. If you really want students to find what they consider to be the most important word, you must give them time to find that word. If students are reading a novel, you might consider having them find the most important word for

MOST IMPORTANT WORD STRATEGY

each chapter. After they've made a list, they can choose the one most important word. Otherwise, choosing the most important from among 50,000 words can be overwhelming!

- **Provide opportunities for students to share and explain their choices.** Students can explain their choice of the most important word in an essay, as Benjamin did, or in several other ways. Some teachers ask students to discuss, in either a small or large group, what they found to be the most important word. Students share their words, explain their reasoning, listen to responses, and then make comments in return. One class using the strategy decided to see if they could reach a consensus on the most important word. First, everyone chose a word. Then, they got into groups of four or five, shared their words, and came up with one word for the group. The class now had five words, which were listed on the board. Each group made a presentation to the class about why its word was the most important. When students voted on the most important word, there was a tie. To break the tie, students wrote persuasive speeches and commercials and made posters that they presented to another class. That class voted on the most important word, based on the presentations. The teacher, therefore, took the strategy to a new level as students learned about good persuasive writing and effective propaganda techniques. The strategy can also be used as an essay question on a test, but that only seems like a fair test item if students have had previous time to reflect on what the most important word is and gather evidence from the text to support their choice.

> *Students share their words, explain their reasoning, listen to responses, and then make comments in return.*

A Few Questions...

1. **Do students always do this in groups?**
   No. I often tell students to think about the text outside of class and to choose the most important word. Then we go around the room and list all their words on the board. Generally, out of a class of twenty-five, you'll have a list of between eight and fifteen different words. At that point, students might get into groups to discuss why they chose their words. I like putting kids that have chosen different words together, but you certainly could put students with the same words into one group so they can discuss various reasons for choosing the same word.

MOST IMPORTANT WORD STRATEGY

2. Does the most important word have to be a word in the text?
That depends on what you want to accomplish. If you want students to infer or generalize, let them choose a word that's not mentioned in the text, but that comes to mind when thinking about the text. I find, though, that students do better with this strategy if I specify that the word must be found in the text.

3. Won't some students just go with a character's name?
If you let them. Remember, many students in middle school and high school read a book through the main character's eyes. They become the main character and live out all the action from that character's point of view, so these students might naturally say that the character's name is the most important. To keep students from doing that, I often tell them that they can't choose a character's name as the most important word.

4. Does that type of restriction mean they always give thoughtful answers?
Not always. When you introduce this strategy, expect a few students to tell you that *of* or *the* or *a* is the most important word because it occurs the most often. It might be that these students feel so overwhelmed by the assignment that they think they can't do it, and the only way out of that embarrassing situation is to make fun of the assignment by coming up with silly answers. You can modify the assignment for these students by having them find the most important chapter, passage, or scene, which they can then narrow to the most important sentence, and finally, to the most important word.

References

Bleich, David. 1975. *Reading and Feelings: An Introduction to Subjective Criticism.* Urbana, Illinois: National Council of Teachers of English.
Cooney, Caroline. 1994. *Driver's Ed.* New York: Delacorte.

MOST IMPORTANT WORD STRATEGY

Most Important Word at a Glance

- After reading a text, students discuss their responses.

- Students decide either independently or in small groups what they think the most important word in the text is, basing their answers on evidence from the text.

- Students share and explain their choices.

PROBABLE PASSAGE STRATEGY

Many readers struggle because they don't predict what a selection might be about and don't think about what they already know about a topic. These students simply open a book, look at words, and begin turning pages. Probable Passage (Wood 1984) is a strategy that helps stop those poor reading habits by encouraging students to make predictions and to activate their prior knowledge about a topic.

Probable Passage is a brief preview of a text from which key words and phrases have been omitted. The teacher chooses these key words from the text and presents them to the students. After discussing what the words mean, students arrange them in categories according to their probable functions in the story (such as Setting, Characters, or Conflicts), then use them to fill in the blanks of the Probable Passage. After reading the actual story, students compare it to their Probable Passages and discuss differences. As students work through this process, they use what they know about story structure, think about vocabulary, and practice making predictions.

Step into a Classroom

A Classroom Model

"Okay, look up here. Here are your words," Ms. Singer said, putting words from Shirley Jackson's short story "Charles" on the overhead projector (see page 44). After Ms. Singer read each word or phrase aloud, she asked students to explain what a *make-believe friend* is and to discuss what a *troublemaker* is.

PROBABLE PASSAGE STRATEGY

home	Laurie	kindergarten	make-believe friend
troublemaker	mom	hits the teacher	mom discovers the truth
throws chalk	says bad words	yells	

Discussing key terms in advance ensured that everyone was familiar with those terms. Then, she uncovered the second part of the transparency, revealing four categories: Setting, Characters, Problem, and Ending. Students arranged the words and phrases in categories. One of the students, Melanie, arranged her words like this:

Setting	Characters	Problem	Ending
home	Laurie	troublemaker	mom discovers the truth
kindergarten	mom	hits the teacher	
	make-believe friend	throws chalk	
		says bad words	
		yells	

Students discussed how they decided to categorize the words and phrases. They spent some time discussing the differences in their responses. Then the teacher presented the following story frame to students:

The setting of the story is _____. _____ is the main character who goes to _____. While there, he invents a _____ who is the _____ at school. The problem in the story is that the troublemaker_____, _____, _____, and _____. The ending of the story is that one day Laurie's _____ goes to school to meet the troublemaker's mom. There _____—her son is the troublemaker!

PROBABLE PASSAGE STRATEGY

Students were told to use the words from their charts to complete the probable passage. Here's what Melanie wrote:

> The setting of the story is <u>home</u>. <u>Laurie</u> is the main character who goes to <u>kindergarten</u>. While there, he invents a <u>make-believe friend</u> who is the <u>troublemaker</u> at school. The problem in the story is that the troublemaker <u>hits the teacher</u>, <u>throws chalk</u>, <u>says bad words</u>, and <u>yells</u>. The ending of the story is that one day Laurie's <u>mom</u> goes to school to meet the troublemaker's mom. There <u>Mom discovers the truth</u>—her son is the troublemaker!

Finally, students read the story and compared it to their Probable Passages. After reading the selection, Melanie made the following comment: "I said that *troublemaker* was a problem word, but after reading the story, I see that Laurie is the troublemaker, so I could have put *troublemaker* in the *Characters* column. But it wouldn't have made too much difference because Laurie being the troublemaker is the problem."

When she was asked if completing the Probable Passage before reading the story helped her understand the story, Melanie replied:

> Yeah, it helped me know what the story was about and what to expect beforehand. At school, sometimes the teacher tells you not to read the back of the book because she wants you to be surprised. But sometimes that means that I don't know what is going to happen, and I like to know what to expect before I read it. So I like filling in what is going to happen because it gives me an idea of what to expect.

What's Going On?

Ms. Singer was using Probable Passage to introduce students to terms and phrases they would encounter while reading and to get them to predict what might happen in the text. As students categorized the words under the headings that Ms. Singer provided, they discussed what the key words and category headings meant. As Melanie explained, the passage

Probable Passage is a powerful prereading strategy and postreading discussion tool.

PROBABLE PASSAGE STRATEGY

"helped me know what the story was about and what to expect beforehand." "Expecting beforehand" is something many readers don't do. Probable Passage, however, encourages students to predict, to discuss and use key words prior to reading the text, and to make comparisons between their Probable Passages and the text. For those reasons, it is a powerful prereading strategy and postreading discussion tool.

Getting the Strategy to Work

- **First, choose key words and write the Probable Passage.** After reading a story, choose the key words, think about what categories are needed, and design a Probable Passage (really just a cloze passage). To choose key words, it is easiest to work backward: Write the Probable Passage, then choose the key words and develop the categories. In the previous example, the teacher had only four categories—Setting, Characters, Problem, and Ending; however, you could use different categories, such as Conflict, Solution, Flashback, Foreshadowing, Symbol, Resolution, or Climax. If you were reading a murder mystery, you might want the categories to be Murderer and Victim. If you were using an expository text, you might have Causes and Effects; Problems and Solutions; or First Event, Second Event, and Third Event. Choose the categories based on the words you've chosen for the Probable Passage.

- **Then, model the strategy a few times.** This means that students need to see you thinking about words, placing them in the correct category, and using them in the Probable Passage. After reading the story, they need to see you discuss how the passage affected your reading of the story.

- **Use Probable Passage before and after reading a selection.** Students begin by arranging the key words into the categories you have provided. After categorizing the key words, students place them within the Probable Passage. At that point, they might change the way they have categorized the words. That's fine. Students then read the text. Some may want to keep their Probable Passages with them as they read. After reading, students compare their Probable Passages with the text and either revise their Probable Passages or just discuss the differences.

In the earlier classroom example, you saw what a struggling reader did after using the strategy only once before. Eventually, the teacher let students generate the passage themselves from key words she provided. Then, the strategy became a Story Impressions strategy (see page 99 of this handbook). Most of the struggling readers, though, did much better when they continued to use this framework because that amount of structure was necessary for success.

PROBABLE PASSAGE STRATEGY

A Few Questions...

1. **How many words should I choose from the story for students to use in a Probable Passage?**
   More than fifteen is usually too many, and less than eight is usually too few. You really need to read the story, select important vocabulary words, think about the Probable Passage frame, decide on the categories, and go from there.

2. **Does everyone need to do a Probable Passage prior to reading a story?**
   Not always. Good readers often know how to use their prior experiences and how to predict what might happen next; therefore, they might not need this structured strategy. Less proficient readers might need some structure but not quite this much. These students would probably benefit from a strategy called Story Impressions (see page 99 of this handbook). Some readers, however, need more structure. They need to look closely at new vocabulary, think about the words in relationship to the story, and fit them into a Probable Passage before seeing them in the text.

3. **Why should students compare their Probable Passages to the story after reading?**
   Students like the guide that Probable Passage provides and will naturally compare what they said would happen with what happened in the story. This comparison leads to interesting discussions. For instance, you can ask questions such as the following: Did your predictions make as much sense as what actually happened? How did your predictions differ from what happened in the story? How did completing the Probable Passage help you understand the story better?

4. **Why is it important to ask students how the strategy helped them understand the story?**
   Struggling readers often say that good readers read fast, read with expression, and know all the words. These readers don't see the "invisible" things that good readers do, such as making predictions, modifying their predictions as they read, and making connections between the text and what they already know. A strategy like Probable Passage makes the invisible visible for them. It forces students to make predictions and to see that sometimes predictions must be modified.

5. **What if the students can't complete the Probable Passage or their predictions just don't match the text at all?**
   If that happens, check the passage you created. The first few passages that I wrote were too difficult for even proficient readers. When I looked closely at the passage, I saw that I had too many terms, too few main ideas, and only single words. Now I try to list around eight to fifteen words, keep my categories broad, and use phrases

PROBABLE PASSAGE STRATEGY

as needed. Plus, I make sure that the Probable Passage uses the category terms. In other words, if Setting is a category, in the Probable Passage I say something very direct, like "The setting of this story is _____."

6. Doesn't the Probable Passage "give away" the story?
The Probable Passage doesn't have to include the conclusion of the story. You can simply end the passage with an earlier event.

References

Wood, Karen D. 1984. Probable Passages: A Writing Strategy. *The Reading Teacher* 37:496–499.

Probable Passage at a Glance

- The teacher chooses key words or phrases from the text students will read, then develops categories for the words and writes the Probable Passage.

- Before students read the text, they arrange the key words and phrases in the categories. Then, they fill in the blanks in the Probable Passage with the key words.

- After students read the text, they discuss how their Probable Passages were similar to or different from the actual text.

RETELLINGS STRATEGY

"So tell me what happened in the story," I asked Easton.

"Well, uh . . . well, it was like this man or, um, this guy, and . . . and they . . . the guy and his, uh brother, goes to . . . uh, well they like leave and then some stuff happens."

Stuff happens. That about summed up the story as far as Easton was concerned. While I'll admit that the general notion that "stuff happens" in a story is accurate, the phrase seems to lack the specificity most of us want in a discussion of a piece of literature. But this level of summary is what many students offer us on a consistent basis. To move students past the "stuff happens" response, consider using a strategy called **Retellings** (Tierney, Readence, and Dishner 1995). A retelling is an oral summary of a text based on a set of story elements, such as setting, main characters, and conflicts. Students use retellings to help them become more specific in their summarizing, to become more organized, to discover main ideas and supporting details, and to become aware of their audience, use of language, and personal responses to texts.

Step into a Classroom

A Classroom Model

It was late September, fifth period. Some of the twenty-eight students were reading silently, others were writing in response journals, and two students, in opposite corners of the classroom, were speaking into tape recorders. They were giving retellings of books they had recently finished reading. One of the

RETELLINGS STRATEGY

students, Amelia, was a struggling reader. While Amelia could read words, she had a lot of difficulty keeping the text organized in her mind. On this day, Amelia gave the following retelling:

> Okay, there are soldiers, and the family, they escape, but the soldiers are going to catch . . . Well, they hide stuff in a casket, and the dogs . . . first she is supposed to take this basket to the boat, and then, like . . . uh . . . the dogs and soldiers stop her, and the basket, it like has hidden stuff—okay—but the cocaine kept the dogs from sniffing it, and then her friend gave her the necklace and she kept it.

This retelling reveals that Amelia has trouble sequencing events as well as organizing her thoughts to present important facts. Her teacher, therefore, began modeling retellings, gave Amelia a rubric, or outline, to follow when giving retellings, and provided her lots of opportunities to practice retellings. Amelia gave the following retelling of Katherine Paterson's *Bridge to Terabithia* in February. The italicized elements are aspects of the retelling that Amelia had worked on specifically.

> It was these two kids, and they wanted, you know, to race. Okay—wait. *This is a retelling for* Bridge to Terabithia *which is about a boy and a girl and, uh . . . they are friends, and, uh, one dies. And it was at the beginning of the school year.* Okay. One of the kids, a boy, his name was Jess and he wanted to win the race so he was like running every day and then at school he met this girl and she was new and they are in the country—*in the country, that is the setting*—and the girl's name is Leslie. *So Jess and Leslie are the main characters, and the setting is the country.* And there are some other characters. Like Marybelle and Jess's parents and his other sisters and Leslie's parents. And so then they become friends, and when they go into the forest over to a little island she says to imagine that he is the king and she is the queen, and they name the land Terabithia, and they like go there to play. He likes it but doesn't tell anyone that they go there. And they are not boyfriend and girlfriend but just friends. And that is like cool. And his dad is mean to him. *That is one of the problems of the story, that his dad doesn't like that he does art, but Jess likes to do art.* And his dad treats his sisters like really nice, and Jess is like, you know, jealous about his dad. So then one day Jess goes with his teacher to look at some art pictures, and Leslie goes to play without him, and she is killed because the bridge to their island is just a tree that has fallen over this creek. Okay. It is really raining and she drowns. And so then Jess has to find out, and he is really sad, and then he is worried it is his fault and stuff, and his dad was almost kind of nice to him—well just a little. *Okay, that's another problem: that Leslie has died. This is like the main problem.*

RETELLINGS STRATEGY

And then Jess takes his little sister there to play, but he makes the bridge safe, and he tells her about Terabithia. And so that is the end. *And the main problem was that Leslie died, and the other problem—but not the main problem—is that Jess's dad doesn't want him to do art.* And there was a bully, but that was earlier, and that was not a main problem.

That's a big difference between September and February. The first retelling has no structure, unity, main ideas, or supporting details. The second one, while certainly not without its problems, is much better.

What's Going On?

Like many struggling readers, Amelia had difficulty recalling what she had read and retelling that information in a logical, coherent manner. However, by comparing Amelia's first retelling in September with the later one in February, we see that after being given a structure to follow, Amelia does have some information that she can share in a logical way. Now her teacher knows that Amelia can absorb information; she just has trouble processing that information in a way that lets her share it with others. The Retellings strategy provides a structure for students who have that difficulty.

Getting the Strategy to Work

Using retellings effectively means modeling retellings often, giving students a rubric they can use to plan and evaluate retellings, evaluating students' retellings over time so students can see growth and areas that need work, and finally, using students' retellings as a way to inform instructional practices.

- **Model several retellings.** Begin by reading a short story or a picture book to students; then retell it. You'll need to have looked over the rubric you want to use and to have practiced this retelling. Next, put a copy of the rubric you want students to use on the overhead projector and discuss your retelling with students. Model a retelling every day for several days, letting students score your retellings. Occasionally, give a poor retelling, making sure you discuss with students what made it poor. Even after students begin giving their own retellings, continue modeling retellings from time to time.

- **Use a rubric to plan and evaluate retellings.** Think of a Retellings rubric as an outline for what you want to see in the retelling. An example of a Retellings rubric appears on page 52. You can also adopt this rubric for your students or write your own. What's important is that students see the rubric before they give their retellings. They shouldn't have to guess what's important. Some teachers let students use the rubric as they give their retellings.

RETELLINGS STRATEGY

Retellings Rubric

Name _____ Date _____

Text _____ Selected by _____

Directions: Use the following checklist to rate the retelling. For each item below, circle a number from 0-3 in the appropriate column. On this scale, 0 means the retelling didn't include the item at all, and 3 means the retelling completely and successfully included the item.

Does this retelling

1. have an introduction that includes the story's title and setting?	0	1	2	3
2. give the characters' names and explain how the characters are related to one another?	0	1	2	3
3. identify the antagonists and protagonists?	0	1	2	3
4. include the main events?	0	1	2	3
5. keep the main events in the correct sequence?	0	1	2	3
6. provide supporting details?	0	1	2	3
7. make sense?	0	1	2	3
8. sound organized?	0	1	2	3
9. discuss the main conflict/problem in the story?	0	1	2	3
10. explain how the main conflict/problem was resolved?	0	1	2	3
11. connect the story to another story or to the reader's life?	0	1	2	3
12. include the reader's personal response to the story?	0	1	2	3

Total Score _____

Comments from listener about the retelling:

Suggestions for the next retelling:

RETELLINGS STRATEGY

- **Evaluate students' progress over time.** For a progress chart to be meaningful, you need to be the one who assesses the retelling plotted on the chart, using the same rubric each time. The following example of a student's progress chart is based on the Retellings rubric shown on page 52. Notice that between Ian's first and ninth retelling, his cumulative score steadily increased, except for January. That makes sense; a lot of time had elapsed between his December and January retellings. But look how quickly his score began climbing again. By February, he was making progress. His last two retellings, both in early May, had scores of 23 and 25.

Name: *Ian*   Class: _____

Retellings Progress Chart

	Sept.	Oct.	Nov.	Dec.	Jan.	Feb.	Mar.	Apr.	May
R13									25
R12									23
R11								20	
R10							18		
R9						17			
R8					13				
R7				16					
R6			14						
R5			12						
R4		9							
R3		8							
R2	7								
R1	6								

ELEMENTS OF LITERATURE   Reading Strategies Handbook

RETELLINGS STRATEGY

- **Use retellings to plan instruction.** Evaluating students' retellings helps you decide what you need to mention to the entire class. For instance, if you notice that several students are not starting their retellings with good introductions, then you know you need to model how to do that. You can also use students' rubrics to help students see what areas they need to work on.

To ensure a successful year with the Retellings strategy, make sure students understand all the components of the rubric, evaluate their scores over time, and use their performance on retellings to plan instruction for individuals and the entire class.

A Few Questions . . .

1. Will retellings help students with their writing?
Yes, if you have used retellings often in the manner described above. If you really want to focus on students' writing, you might want to look at Hazel Brown and Brian Cambourne's book *Read and Retell* (1990). With their approach, retellings are always written, and the focus of the retelling is on the author's craft. I don't suggest using this approach with struggling readers, however, until they understand the art of retelling.

2. How do you listen to all of the retellings?
You need to reduce the number of retellings you listen to. First, think about who needs to be doing retellings. Students who can already find the main idea and supporting details, organize their thoughts about a text, and relate events in the correct sequence don't need this strategy. Second, when you start a new strategy, start small. Choose five or six students from one class, have them record their retellings on a cassette tape, and listen to them later. Third, you don't need to listen to all the retellings. Listen to one or two a month. At other times, let students score each other's retellings or score their own from recordings they make.

3. How many retellings should students be doing?
How often students do retellings is up to you. One teacher had her students read silently for the first ten minutes of class on Mondays, Tuesdays, and Wednesdays. On Thursdays and Fridays they got with a partner and did a retelling during that first ten minutes. The more often students have a chance to practice the strategy, the better the results.

4. As students keep practicing, should I keep modeling?
As students learn the strategy, you will need to model less often. I'd suggest, though, that you model retellings as students encounter new types of text structures. For instance, if students will be reading a selection that has a

RETELLINGS STRATEGY

flashback, those who don't understand how to sequence will not know how to retell the selection without seeing it modeled.

References

Brown, Hazel, and Brian Cambourne. 1990. *Read and Retell.* Portsmouth, N.H.: Heinemann Publishers.

Tierney, Robert J., John E. Readence, and Ernest K. Dishner. 1995. *Reading Strategies and Practices: A Compendium.* 4th ed. Needham Heights, Mass.: Allyn and Bacon.

Retellings at a Glance

- The teacher models a retelling by reading a brief story and retelling it to students. Then, the class evaluates and discusses the teacher's retelling using a rubric.

- Using a rubric, students plan and evaluate their retellings.

- The teacher assesses students' progress over time by plotting their scores on a chart.

SAVE THE LAST WORD FOR ME STRATEGY

"What do you want to say about the story?" I asked Josh.

"Nothin'," he responded.

I waited. Nothing happened.

"You're sure?" I asked.

"I've got nothin' to say," he responded, never bothering to look at me.

I was disappointed but not actually surprised. Josh struggled through texts and often felt he had nothing to say about what he had read. Once, in a moment of rare talkativeness, Josh explained why he sometimes had nothing to say: "Why do you keep on askin' me that? I mean, I got nothin' to say. You keep on askin' me, and why? I mean, I used to have somethin' to say, but it wasn't ever right, so why did the teacher even ask me if it was always wrong?"

I have to agree with Josh: Who wants to be told continually that their answers are wrong? Some readers, though, often face just that situation. They either can't answer the questions, so they never try, or they risk an answer, only to discover that their answer is wrong. Eventually, they learn to distrust their own responses, and finally they don't even bother to form them. When that happens, we must convince these students to trust their ability to form responses and to recognize that all readers—including good readers—constantly refine their responses based on what they already know, what they learn from the text and from others. One strategy that helps readers learn to

SAVE THE LAST WORD FOR ME STRATEGY

trust their own responses while learning from others' responses is called **Save the Last Word for Me** (Short, Harste, and Burke 1996).

Save the Last Word for Me requires students to choose a portion of a text that they particularly like and to copy that text onto the front of a note card. On the back of the card, students explain what that sentence or passage means to them. Next, students get in small groups and share their passages. The listeners respond to the passage by saying what it means to them. After everyone has finished making comments, the student who wrote the comment turns the card over and shares what he or she has written. At that point, no one can refute, add to, change, or argue with what is said. The last word belongs to that student.

Step into a Classroom

A Classroom Model

The students entered the classroom noisily. Some talked to their friends; others just looked bored. No one was getting ready for the day's work. No one seemed aware that the tardy bell had rung or that this classroom was any different from the one they had just left. These students weren't just reluctant readers; they were reluctant students. Many of them approached all of their classes with the same goal—to do as little as possible.

"Okay, folks. Now," the teacher said loudly over the twenty-three voices still talking. A few students rotated to face forward in their desks.

"Folks. Now," Mr. Johnson continued. The class settled down some more. "Who remembers what we did yesterday?" he asked.

Long pause. Students shifted uncomfortably in their chairs.

"Oh yeah, you know, that stuff to read and then find a good part," one student finally offered.

"Right. Get your books and open them to page 283," Mr. Johnson said, nodding his head.

Students opened their books as Mr. Johnson started distributing 4- x 6-inch index cards. "Remember we read this on Monday and Tuesday." A few students nodded their heads. "Now, last night you were going to look through the text and find a sentence or maybe two or three sentences that you liked a lot for some reason. Maybe it was funny, or what they were saying meant a lot to you,

SAVE THE LAST WORD FOR ME STRATEGY

or it explained something. Okay, then. Who's got their sentences?" About half the hands in the classroom went up. "On the front of the card, write the sentence or sentences that you found; then, turn it over and write why you liked those sentences. You can start by saying, 'I chose these sentences because . . .' Those of you who haven't found your sentences, you've got fifteen minutes."

"What do we copy down?" one student called out.

"What do we write? Something we think?" another asked.

Mr. Johnson patiently answered each question while moving toward the overhead projector at the front of the room.

"This is easy, folks, so listen. Now." His raised voice resulted in absolute quiet. "See this?" he said, putting a transparency on the overhead that pictured the front of a note card. "We've done this before. Think about what you did. On the front you copied a sentence or a few sentences. Then, on the back," he said, pointing to the second card on the transparency, "you write what those sentences mean to you."

"Oh yeah, we did this," one or two students said.

"Yeah, and then we get the last word?" another student asked. Mr. Johnson just nodded.

Those students began to write. The other students began looking through the text. Eventually the students who were writing were finished. Mr. Johnson directed them to move into groups of two or three, to share their passages, to listen to what the others had to say about their passages, and finally, to read their own comments about the passages.

Here's a portion of a conversation that begins after one student, Jake, has read what he copied from the textbook:

"That was good," Nikki said.

"Yeah," Jasmine agreed.

"That was a good part where it said that the wind pushed through them like knives," Derek said.

"I didn't get that," Nikki said.

"You know, like how a knife goes through stuff, like slicin'? That was it—the wind was like a knife," Derek explained.

"Oh," Nikki said.

No one said anything. Finally, Jasmine said, "So, Jake, um, you get the last word."

"Okay." Jake read from the back of the card, "This was good. The way the author wrote it, I could see it really good. I liked it because the way it said the knife is like the wind I could really imagine it a lot."

Another group's conversation was proceeding like this:

SAVE THE LAST WORD FOR ME STRATEGY

"So that's what I put," Katrina said after she finished reading what was on the front of her card. "Anyone got somethin' to say?" she asked.

"That's good," Sonia said.

"Uh-huh," Monique agreed.

"I thought that part meant he was bein' bad, and so it confused me," Nolene said. "I was thinkin' he was good until that part, you know?"

"Why bad?" Sonia said.

"Like where it says he upset them all the time. It wouldn't be sayin' that if he weren't bein' bad. Before that I thought he was good," she explained.

No one said anything for a minute. Katrina started grinning. "That's what I say, too. Here listen, I say that this part means he was just actin' good, but if you look close, then he was bad. I like the way the story makes him look good, but then you just get this feelin' that he's bad."

"But—" Sonia began; however, Katrina cut her off.

"Nope. It's my last word," Katrina said, still smiling.

What's Going On?

This is a challenging class. Many of us will never teach a class like this one, and just as many of us have probably taught this class more often than we care to remember. These are the kids who sometimes anger us the quickest, yet often tug at our hearts the most. Often very likable teens, they lack the school skills that so many of their counterparts possess. Lacking those skills, they find school a place where they continually confront their own failure. Many of these students find that the best way to handle that failure is to act as if failure is meaningless to them, so they fall back on bravado, flip remarks, and apathy.

Students are willing to participate in Save the Last Word for Me because it allows each voice to be heard and, at the same time, gives each participant the opportunity to be the authority. In the dialogue above, Sonia tried to respond to Katrina's Last Word comment. Katrina cut her off, announcing, "Nope. It's my last word." The goal, of course, is for these students to be willing eventually to hear other ideas or dissenting opinions. This strategy helps students take the first steps toward that goal.

These struggling readers were doing something they rarely did. They were finding a passage in a text that was meaningful to them, listening to what others had to say about that text, and then offering their opinions unchallenged. Without doubt, the conversations lacked the depth and exploratory nature we would hope to hear from secondary students; however, the students, despite their ages, read at an elementary level and had little experience shaping a response to literature. The fact that they were willing to do this, to rec-

SAVE THE LAST WORD FOR ME STRATEGY

ognize that they did have something to say about a text, was a big step forward for them. As Derek later explained, "I say what it means last. I can't be wrong." For students who have rarely given themselves the opportunity to volunteer any response, Save the Last Word for Me provides a scaffold that encourages safe risk taking.

> *Save the Last Word for Me provides a scaffold that encourages safe risk taking.*

Getting the Strategy to Work

This strategy is fairly simple to explain, requires minimal modeling, and can be partially completed outside of the classroom. Here are the steps to follow as you introduce the strategy for the first time:

- **First, explain the strategy by actually doing it with students.** Before you begin a discussion of a text with your students, prepare a Last Word card. On the front, write your favorite sentence or passage from the text; on the back, explain why you chose that passage and why you think it is significant. Toward the end of the discussion, tell the class that you are going to share with them a passage that you particularly liked, that they will have a chance to say whatever they want to say about that passage, that you will read what you want to say about it, and at that point, they can add nothing! Then, read the card and ask students to comment. Don't be surprised if a lot of students don't respond to what you wrote; remember, these are students who believe response is risky.

- **Second, have your students prepare their Last Word cards.** They can use either the same story that you used to model the strategy or another story. Do this soon after you model the strategy or you will have to begin again. You might consider having students identify the important passage at home and then discuss the passage in class. Be sure to keep extra blank cards in the classroom. If some students don't have a card to share with the group, don't allow them to participate in the Save the Last Word for Me discussion. Instead, have them write an essay about why their chosen passage is important. That usually happens only once before students make sure they are prepared.

- **Third, have students share their passages and comments.** Since the focus of this strategy is letting students have the last word, they've got to have some in-class time for discussions. Reading, choosing passages, and preparing cards can all be done outside of class, but the sharing and responding must be done in class. Because this strategy is a good prewriting strategy, you might sometimes have students write their responses, using their own initial comments

SAVE THE LAST WORD FOR ME STRATEGY

as well as what other students have said about their passages. These written responses can then be evaluated. You can also evaluate the strategy by giving a participation grade, looking at students' passages and responses on their cards, and comparing their responses over time.

As students share passages, listen to others, and respond without fear of being told they are wrong, they begin to build confidence in themselves as readers and responders. As students choose meaningful passages from the text, they are analyzing and evaluating. As they write about why they chose that passage, they are learning to explain their responses to a text. As they listen to what other students have to say about the same passage, they are learning to appreciate various points of view. They know that they eventually get to explain their points of view and, therefore, don't feel the need to argue their points. For those reasons, Save the Last Word for Me is a strategy that is effective for struggling readers.

> *As students share passages, listen to others, and respond without fear of being told they are wrong, they begin to build confidence in themselves as readers and responders.*

A Few Questions . . .

1. **Do students use Save the Last Word for Me just to improve their confidence?**
   No. While that would be a good thing to do for these students, the strategy does much more than that. As students look for the passage in the text that is the most meaningful to them, they are rereading (a great thing for all readers to do), comparing and contrasting (Why is this section more or less meaningful than another section?), and learning to articulate why it is meaningful. They develop their listening skills as they learn to listen to someone else's response to what they've written. Furthermore, the strategy can help you teach literary elements. If you want students to focus on descriptive writing, simply tell them to find the descriptive writing that they like the best. If you want them to focus on theme or conflict, tell them to find the passage that best explains the theme or conflict. This strategy can have as few or as many parameters as you want.

2. **Do students really need to write down their responses?**
   Yes. This time, unlike some of the other strategies, students really need to commit their thoughts to paper. Without that commitment, they often write down a passage without figuring out why they like it.

SAVE THE LAST WORD FOR ME STRATEGY

3. **What if students write one thing down but, after listening to others, change their minds?**

    That happens. And if you believe that meaning is in part derived from the community of readers, then you should expect that to happen. Explain to students that when they read from the backs of their cards, it is perfectly acceptable to say something like, "Here's what I wrote, but now, after listening to so-and-so, I'd like to make some additions or changes." Students then get the added bonus of explaining how listening to another student affected their thinking.

4. **What if students just pick any passage and say that they liked it best?**

    You can prevent that by requiring students to include at least two reasons for liking a passage best. Tell students that they may *not* say they chose a certain passage just because they liked it. "Tell me *why* you liked it," I constantly remind them.

5. **What if a student really wants to say something after someone else has had the last word?**

    No can do! Part of the strategy is its title: Save the Last Word for Me. However, you should always modify strategies to fit your class's needs. If you see that students want to continue the discussion after someone has had the last word, tell them that this time, the dialogue can continue after the last word has been shared. Just realize that you are modifying the strategy and losing one of its benefits.

6. **So what are the benefits again?**

    Save the Last Word for Me gives struggling readers the chance to form responses without the worry of being told they are wrong. It also encourages them to look closely at a text, choose a part that is meaningful to them, listen to what others say about their choice, and articulate first in writing and then orally why that text is important to them.

References

Short, Kathy Gnagey, Jerome C. Harste, and Carolyn L. Burke. 1996. *Creating Classrooms for Authors and Inquirers.* 2d ed. Portsmouth, N.H.: Heinemann Publishers.

SAVE THE LAST WORD FOR ME STRATEGY

Save the Last Word for Me at a Glance

- After reading a text, students prepare a Last Word card, writing their favorite passage from the text on the front of the card and why they liked it on the back.

- In small groups, students take turns reading the quotations on their cards, allowing other members of the group to respond, and then reading their "last words" from the back of the card.

SAY SOMETHING STRATEGY

Have you ever asked students to discuss their responses to a piece of literature, only to hear a conversation like this?

Gary: You first.

Lonnie: Not me. [*long pause*]

Gary: You going to tonight's game?

Lonnie: Yeah. You?

Gary: Yeah.

Often readers struggle because while they read, their eyes move over the words, but their minds move to thoughts of weekend plans, last night's phone conversations, or after-school sports events. They don't focus on what they are reading. To help those students break that habit, we need to help them attend to what they are reading. One very simple strategy that keeps readers focused on the text is called **Say Something.**

Say Something (Harste, Short, and Burke 1988) is a during-reading strategy in which students occasionally pause and "say something" to a partner about what they've just read. They either make a prediction, ask a question, make a comment, or make a connection. Students who are paying attention to what they read have something to say; they say it and move on. Students who reach a designated stopping place and find they have nothing to say suddenly have a very strong signal that they need to return to the text and reread.

SAY SOMETHING STRATEGY

Step into a Classroom

A Classroom Model

Everyone in the fifth-period English class was reading. Really reading. No one was writing notes or doodling in margins. No combing hair or filing nails. No trying to do math homework, digging through backpacks, or making trips to the pencil sharpener. Just reading. Suddenly a student tapped another on the shoulder and whispered, "You there yet?" When the other said yes, their heads bent close and some whispering began.

Josie: I'll go first.

Luci: Okay.

Josie: I didn't get it until this part here. [*She points to the second paragraph of "The Tell-Tale Heart."*] See this where he says, "You fancy me mad"? Well, then I thought, I get it—he is crazy. And then I decided at this part here that this is taking place a long time ago because see, he is using a lantern, and I thought maybe this was like in Western times.

Luci: I don't think so. He doesn't sound like a rancher or anything. But I think he is crazy. Do you think that when he says "his Evil Eye" he means the man is evil? Like maybe that is his name. See how it's in capital letters?

Josie: Uh-uh. I don't think so. I think like you say "Don't give me the evil eye," that the guy was giving him the evil eye, so he's like calling his eye that. Uh, did you know this word?

Luci: What?

Josie: This: *dis-sim-u-la-tion*.

Luci: Uh-uh. But it says he was being cautious, so I guess it is like being careful.

Josie: You done?

Luci: Yeah. You?

Josie: Uh-huh.

Josie and Luci went back to reading. At the same time they were having their conversation, two other students had also stopped reading.

Bruce: I just don't get it.

Eric: Get what?

Bruce: Any of it. Like here—what does this mean? "Object there was none. Passion there was none."

Eric: I guess I didn't see that part. [*Eric starts to reread. Looks up.*] Give me just a minute.

SAY SOMETHING STRATEGY

These quiet conversations continued throughout the room as students read, stopped, talked, and then continued reading. Occasionally, students like Eric could be seen turning back a few pages and rereading. Sometimes students jotted down notes on a piece of paper. Most conversations lasted three to four minutes. As the students read and talked, the teacher circulated through the room with a clipboard, listening to conversations, sometimes answering questions, but mostly just taking notes. After about thirty minutes the teacher stopped the students and reminded them that as they finished the story at home, they should continue stopping to say something. "If you don't have anything to say, go back and reread. You missed something. If you come up with a question you can't answer, jot it down. We'll talk about it tomorrow."

What's Going On?

Say Something helps students think about what they are reading by helping them see where they aren't paying attention. In the example above, Eric rereads the text after his partner points out some sentences that Eric had just breezed over. Josie and Luci attempt to create the setting and to understand an unfamiliar word.

The purpose of Say Something is to help students comprehend what they are reading by helping them stay focused. Telling students to say something about the text, or, as I've found, giving them specific types of things they can say, keeps students interacting with the text. From that interaction comes meaning. And that's the goal, isn't it?

> *Say Something helps students think about what they are reading by helping them see where they aren't paying attention.*

Getting the Strategy to Work

- **First, model the strategy.** If you can recruit a colleague to help you, demonstrate a Say Something to students. You and your colleague read a brief passage and then pause and say something about what you've read. Make sure you say a range of things—from asking very specific questions, such as how to say a certain word, to making very general comments, such as saying what the passage reminds you of. If you can't find someone to join you for a moment or two, then type out your dialogue instead, make a transparency of it, and put it on the overhead projector.

- **Explain the rules to students.** After you "show" a Say Something, go over the rules (which you can put on a poster and hang in the room) until students get the idea of how to do the strategy. You can either choose the points

SAY SOMETHING STRATEGY

in the text where you want students to stop to say something, or have students decide for themselves where to stop. Tell students that when they stop to say something (after every three to four paragraphs or so), they must either make a prediction, ask a question, make a comment, or make a connection. These four general areas give them enough direction to help them begin the conversations with their partners, yet allow enough latitude for their own needs to emerge.

Rules for Say Something

1. With your partner, decide who will say something first.

2. When you say something, you may do one of the following:

   You can make a prediction.

   You can ask a question.

   You can make a comment.

   You can make a connection.

3. If you can't do one of those four things, then you need to reread.

You can explain the four response categories to students by telling them the following:

When you do your Say Somethings, there are four things you can say. You can say what you think might happen next. That's called a prediction. You make a prediction by saying, "I think that such and such will happen" or "I predict that . . . ." You can ask a question. If you don't know a word, don't understand a sentence, or feel confused about what is happening, then ask a question. If you don't want to make a prediction or ask a question, then you can make a comment. This can be a comment about what you like or don't like, what you don't understand, what you think is interesting, or what you think about what is happening. Finally, you can make a connection. That means you can say, "This reminds me of . . ." or "This story is like . . ." or "This character makes me think about . . . ."

SAY SOMETHING STRATEGY

- **Provide opportunities for practice.** Students first need to practice using Say Something on very short texts—just a few paragraphs or short poems. This allows them to become familiar with the strategy before they start using it with assignments. You may wish to have students use a simple chart such as the one on page 70 to help them keep track of their Say Something comments.

A Few Questions . . .

1. **Should students be allowed to choose their partners?**
   Sometimes yes, sometimes no. Make sure that students understand that this is work time, not visit time. If I see students together and know that they are saying something about anything other than the text, then they know they've lost the privilege to work together again for a while. It's a good idea, however, to try to let friends work together. Secondary students are so connected to their friends that putting them with someone they never spend time with almost assures failure for the strategy.

2. **Should everyone do a Say Something?**
   No. After students have used the strategy enough to see that it really does help them understand what they read, then students who don't have trouble staying focused can choose whether or not to use the strategy.

3. **Is the strategy graded?**
   You can't get a 100 percent or an 88 percent on a Say Something. Students are more willing to do something, however, if they believe that they are getting graded, so I give participation grades. Plus, I have students reflect on their own Say Somethings after about every third one by having them answer these questions:
   a. How has using Say Something changed how you read?
   b. What's something you discovered through Say Something about the story you just finished?
   c. What types of comments do you make the least often and the most often?
   d. What do you want to do to make your Say Somethings more effective?
   e. What do you need me to do to help you with your Say Somethings?

4. **Can Say Something be done without a partner?**
   It certainly works best with a partner, but it can be done alone. Reread what Mrs. Leiper told her class to do at home. It also can be done at school as a Say Something . . . Silently. Wallis (1998) explains that Say Something . . . Silently "provides students with feedback in situations where a partner isn't available" and is "particularly helpful as an independent reading . . . strategy." With this variation students "plan where [they] will stop and say something [to themselves] or write something about what [they] just read."

ELEMENTS OF LITERATURE   Reading Strategies Handbook   **69**

SAY SOMETHING STRATEGY

5. So what's the overall goal of Say Something?
The goal of Say Something is to increase students' understanding of the text by helping them to pay attention to the text. Having students stop to make comments or ask questions about what they are reading engages them in a dialogue with the text. As a result of this conversation, students create meaning.

Say Something Chart

Prediction	Comment	Question	Connection

References

Harste, Jerome C., Kathy Gnagey Short, and Carolyn L. Burke. 1988. *Creating Classrooms for Authors: The Reading-Writing Connection.* Portsmouth, N.H.: Heinemann Publishers.

Wallis, John. 1998. Strategies: What Connects Readers to Meaning. In *Into Focus: Understanding and Creating Middle School Readers,* edited by Kylene Beers and Barbara J. Samuels. Norwood, Mass.: Christopher-Gordon Publishers.

Say Something at a Glance

- The teacher models the strategy by "saying something" about a text with a colleague or by reading and discussing a typed Say Something dialogue with students.

- Students read a short text, stopping occasionally to discuss the text with a partner. In their conversations, students must make a prediction, ask a question, make a comment, or make a connection.

- Students practice Say Somethings using very short texts before using the strategy with assignments.

SCALES STRATEGY

There are fish scales, piano scales, the famous scales of justice, and the dreaded bathroom scales. There are also scales that help students make sense of the texts they read. These scales help students make comparisons, draw conclusions, and respond to generalizations about the text. They are particularly beneficial for students who need assistance organizing their thoughts or who benefit from seeing information arranged in a graphic form. Scales are primarily a postreading tool; however, they could be used before reading as part of an Anticipation Guide (see page 17 for a discussion of Anticipation Guides) or during reading to help students see changes as the plot and characters develop.

Likert Scales (Johnson and Louis 1987) require students to decide how much they agree or disagree with a statement. **Semantic Differential Scales** (Johnson and Louis 1987) require students to choose a word or phrase that best describes a character. **Comparison Grids** (Johnson and Louis 1987) allow students to rate one or more characters on two traits at once.

Step into a Classroom

A Classroom Model

"What'd you put?" the tall fourteen-year-old boy asked the girl sitting beside him.

"I put *strongly agree*. What'd you say?" the girl asked.

"Strongly agree? How'd you get that?" he said. "I put *disagree*."

SCALES STRATEGY

"Disagree? How could you disagree? Of course he disturbed the universe; that's what he did the whole book," she said, tapping the item on the Likert Scale that said, "In spite of the book's ending, Jerry did disturb the universe."

"Aw, come on. He's bleeding his guts out on the football field at the end and telling his so-called friend to never disturb the universe and saying that they won. They've probably killed him. And nothing's changed at the school. The teachers still don't care what Archie and his gang are doing, and Brother Leon is still as mean as ever. What got disturbed?"

"He made a statement. He stuck by his principles. He never gave in," she responded.

"Sure, he gave in, right here at the end," he said, opening his book to the last page. "Plus, you can't disturb the universe if nothing changes. Think of it this way: If you do something to somebody and that person doesn't notice it, then you didn't disturb them. Only when they notice it did you disturb them."

"No, not really," said another boy sitting across from them. "Sometimes people disturb me, and I just don't want to let on that they are bothering me, so I just sit still."

"Yeah, but then they really didn't disturb you enough to change anything," the first boy replied. No one said anything for a minute, then he asked, "What'd you put for the next one?" and the conversation continued.

After hearing these students discuss the Likert Scale they had completed for Robert Cormier's *The Chocolate War*, I talked with their teacher about her students' experiences using scales. What pleased her most about the conversation was that the boy leading the discussion had two months earlier sat in discussion groups and never said a word.

"What changed?" I asked, after hearing about this young man's previous behavior.

"I was using a lot of novel guides that had questions for each chapter, and most of the time he wouldn't do those. When I asked him why, he said, 'What's the use? I'd just get all the answers wrong anyway.' After I started using Likert Scales, he told me that they seemed more opinion based, so how could he get them wrong? Now kids talk more about why they've marked what they did, and with more talk going on, the kids are learning more about the book."

"So are you saying that Likert Scales made him a better reader?" I asked.

"He still has reading problems, but he is talking more about what he has read, so he's just more interested. The Likert Scales have made him think more about what he's reading, and that is what is helping him understand better."

SCALES STRATEGY

What's Going On?

The teacher was correct; students were talking a lot about the book, and they were offering their opinions. When I asked students in the class what they thought about using Likert Scales, one said, "I like them. They are easier than real questions because you don't have to look through the story for just one right word for an answer, but you get to use your mind." Another said, "They are okay. Some are pretty hard because you don't know what the right answer should be, and you can't find it in the book." These students are right—responding to items on a scale is both easier and harder than responding to typical questions because the answer must come from their own minds.

Scales encourage students to think about and discuss what they've read. In addition, as students discuss the reasons for their choices, they draw conclusions, make inferences and generalizations, make comparisons, and use the text to support their opinions.

> *Scales encourage students to think about and discuss what they've read.*

Getting the Strategy to Work

The best way to teach scales is to complete a scale for students. After you've read something together (anything from a selection in students' anthologies to a picture book), complete a scale, making sure to explain how you arrived at your opinions based on evidence from the text. What's important to remember with scales is that students must explain their choices.

Likert Scales require students to read a statement and decide how much they agree or disagree with the statement. Students mark with an X or circle the term that indicates their level of agreement with the statement. Likert Scales often focus on generalizations about characters, theme, conflicts, or

---

In spite of the book's ending, Jerry did disturb the universe.

| Strongly Agree | Agree | Disagree | Strongly Disagree |

Explanation: _____

SCALES STRATEGY

symbolism. The best items don't have clear-cut answers found in the book. For instance, if you've read *The Chocolate War,* then you know Brother Leon is a despicable character. Therefore, you shouldn't write an item that says, "Brother Leon is mean," but instead should write, "Brother Leon is a realistic character in this book." Now students have something to talk about. And that's what you want the scale to do—stimulate discussion.

Semantic Differential Scales place opposite character traits (such as strong-weak) at opposite ends of a scale, then ask students to decide how much of the trait a character possesses. These scales focus on character development and can be used to track character changes through a story. The Semantic Differential Scale below has students consider how strong or weak a person Jerry is. If students choose the far left circle, they are saying Jerry has a lot of strength; if they choose the far right circle, they are saying he is very weak. Other circles represent those two traits to a lesser degree. What makes this such a good item is that students could make a case for choosing any of the circles, since Jerry acts weak at times and strong at other times. The issue, as with the Likert Scale, isn't whether students mark the correct circle but why they make their choices. Students can use the scale to track character development by rating a character both at the beginning and at the end of the story.

Jerry Renault is

strong   weak
○   ○   ○   ○   ○

Explanation: _____
_____
_____
_____
_____

SCALES STRATEGY

	very powerful	powerful	neither	weak	very weak
very bad	Captain Flint				
bad	Long John Silver				
neither					
good		Dr. Livesay		Jim Hawkins	
very good					

Comparison Grids, like Semantic Differential Scales, also focus on character development, but they can be used to rate characters on several traits at once. Comparison Grids use pairs of opposite qualities, such as kind-mean and wise-foolish. Of course, you can use any pair of words you choose. Students who have trouble making comparisons should find the Comparison Grid helpful, since it allows them to visualize trait differences. These students might also benefit from filling in the grid as they read a text rather than waiting until the end. For instance, you could tell students that as they read a text, they will be comparing two characters and deciding which one is kinder and which is wiser. They will plot how much kindness and wisdom each of those characters has on the Comparison Grid. Some students find it helpful to do this several times throughout the text. They can use several grids, plot in different colors, or write *B* (beginning), *M* (middle), and *E* (end) next to the character's name on the grid as they read.

Whichever type of scale you decide to use, remember that as students make their choices, they will be analyzing, synthesizing, and evaluating information. They will be making inferences, making comparisons, and drawing conclusions. And they will be using their knowledge of the text to explain their decisions.

> *As students make their choices, they will be analyzing, synthesizing, and evaluating information.*

ELEMENTS OF LITERATURE

SCALES STRATEGY

A Few Questions...

1. **How do I know what kind of scale to use?**
   Think about your objective. If you want students to analyze a single character, use a Semantic Differential Scale. If you want students to compare two characters or characters from more than one story, you might want a Comparison Grid. If you want students to decide how much they agree or disagree with statements that are generalizations about a story, use a Likert Scale. More important than the type of scale you use, though, are the statements or pairs of words that you choose. Use word pairings or statements that require reflection and that have no obvious "better" choice. (There are several word pairs that work well for many characters, such as strong-weak, kind-mean, brave-cowardly, honest-dishonest, bold-shy, wise-foolish, and selfish-unselfish.)

2. **How many items should I include on each scale?**
   Ten items—a favorite number for many teachers—can be too many. Remember, the point of the scale is for students to defend their answers. Scales that have four to six items are more manageable.

3. **What should students do after completing the scales?**
   In the previous classroom example, students discussed and defended their responses in small groups. They could also write about or create visual images of their responses, stage debates with others who had different opinions, interview each other about their responses, or write editorials about the characters. These are only a few ideas, however; there are many other follow-up activities that students could do.

4. **How should I assess students' responses to the scales?**
   You are evaluating their reasons for their responses. I assess on a three-point scale:

   1 = Your explanation didn't even begin to convince me.
   2 = I'm somewhat convinced, but still a little hesitant.
   3 = I buy into everything you've said!

   Struggling readers often need guidelines on how to complete the scale, so you may want to tell them how many reasons to provide. For this to work, you need to give them examples of 1, 2, and 3 responses; so when you teach scales, make sure to model each type of explanation.

SCALES STRATEGY

References

Johnson, Terry D., and Daphne R. Louis. 1987. *Literacy through Literature.* Portsmouth, N.H.: Heinemann Publishers.

Scales at a Glance

- The teacher chooses and writes a scale based on the desired learning objective (for example, comparing two characters in a story). Students complete a Likert Scale to respond to generalizations about the story, a Semantic Differential Scale to analyze characters, or a Comparison Grid to compare characters from different stories.

- After reading a text, students complete the scale, explaining their choices using specific evidence from the text.

- Students share their responses in a small-group discussion, debate, or other activity.

SKETCH TO STRETCH STRATEGY

Before I began using strategies with students, I used to ask them to do things like write about the theme of a story, write a paragraph about the symbolism in "The Scarlet Ibis," or—my personal favorite—express a generalization about the story that can be applied to their lives. Guess what I got: Many of my students struggled just to get through the story. They had trouble with the difficult words, the syntax, the complicated plots. Students' reading experiences became even more frustrating when I asked them to describe their responses to the text. They would be honest and say things like, "I know what the story is about, and I know what it means—I just don't know how to tell you."

What I found out was that the ideas these students could express visually were far beyond what I had ever imagined they could express. By formulating images using a strategy called Sketch to Stretch, students began talking about symbols and about what the text meant to them. For some students, putting ideas into pictures, rather than words, is the best way to express responses to a text.

Sketch to Stretch (Harste and Burke 1988) is a postreading strategy in which students think about what a passage or entire selection means to them and then draw symbolic representations of their interpretations of the text. As students discuss the text and decide what to draw, they think about the theme, draw conclusions, form generalizations, recognize cause-and-effect relationships, and summarize.

SKETCH TO STRETCH STRATEGY

Step into a Classroom

A Classroom Model

Thursday afternoon, mid-October. Most of the students were in class before the bell rang. (As one student told me, "If you miss the first five minutes of Ms. Garza's class, you've missed about a year's worth of information.") All of the students had failed the reading portion of last year's standardized test.

The teacher was at the front of the room arranging some transparencies. The bell rang for class to begin, and Ms. Garza started talking before the echo of the ring was gone.

"Okay, everyone, look at this. What do you think?" she asked, putting on the overhead projector a transparency of a heart such as one would draw for Valentine's Day.

"Not much is what I think," someone from the back of the room said. Everyone laughed.

"I agree," Ms. Garza said, smiling. "But check this out," she said, changing transparencies. Now she had an interesting picture: a ripped-apart heart that had a large snake wrapped in and around it. In the snake's mouth was a small glass tube with a clear liquid dripping out of it.

"Now that's cool," someone else said.

"Yes," Ms. Garza said. "This is Jason's drawing from last year when we read *Romeo and Juliet,* a play about a romance that has a few problems."

"I'd say it has problems," a girl in the front said. "It looks like it has real problems, and I bet it has some dead people."

"You're right. Now look at this one," Ms. Garza said as she changed transparencies. This time she showed a picture of a large tree with a nest

SKETCH TO STRETCH STRATEGY

on one branch. In the nest were several baby birds, and when you looked closely, there was also a person—the upper body and face of a grown man—who, from the red smear on his chest, appeared to have been wounded. At the bottom of the picture was the following statement: "This is my sketch for *To Kill a Mockingbird*. It is a nest of mockingbirds, and Boo Radley is in it, too, because he is a mockingbird, something that shouldn't get killed–like Atticus told to Scout–because they don't do any hurt to anyone. Boo didn't get shot in the book, but he was always getting hurt because he was different."

After a moment, a girl said, "I get it. Boo is like a mockingbird. I don't know why he was different, but whatever it was, it was hurting him. That is so cool, that picture."

This continued for a few more minutes as Ms. Garza showed more sketches and students made comments. Finally, Ms. Garza stopped and told the students that the pictures had been drawn by her students from last year after they had read a novel or a selection from their literature books. "It is part of a strategy called Sketch to Stretch," she explained. "You read something, find something in what you read that is important to you, and then draw a picture that symbolizes what it meant to you."

"So we gotta draw the story," one boy said, frowning.

"No. Look at this one again," Ms. Garza said, returning to the *To Kill a Mockingbird* picture. "You haven't read this yet, but I promise you there is no scene in the book when a grown man crawls up into a bird's nest. Steve drew it this way because it symbolized how he thought Boo, a character in the book, felt."

No one said anything for a moment, and then someone asked how Steve knew what to draw.

SKETCH TO STRETCH STRATEGY

"He thought of it himself," Ms. Garza explained. "As he read the book he started getting ideas about what was important to him. Then he created his sketch."

No response—which was a good response. No moans, just silence. "Okay," Ms. Garza began, "let's try it ourselves. Last night you finished 'Top Man' and . . ."

"I didn't get it," a young man on the third row said.

"Me neither, like he died but then his ax was there or . . ."

"Save your comments," Ms. Garza said, "until you get with your partner. This first time for this Sketch to Stretch, I want you to work with a partner. No pictures of just a mountain with a man on top. Instead, draw a sketch of what the story means to you. On the back of your sketch, jot down why you drew what you did. Work with a partner, but when you start drawing, if you want, you can each draw your own picture. I'm going to give you twenty-five minutes. You've got approximately thirty seconds to get with one partner and to start work, or I will assign partners."

Noise erupted as everyone immediately got a partner. Students pushed desks close together, looked through backpacks for literature books, hunted down pencils, and began talking about the story. As they did that, Ms. Garza distributed white paper for their drawings. "If I can hear your voice," Ms. Garza said over their talk, "you are too loud." The confusion settled, and soon a low rumble of voices and turning pages were all that could be heard. At the back of the room, two students who hadn't said anything all class period began talking about the story.

"So what do you want to draw?" Jack asked the other student.

"I don't know," Gayle replied.

Silence for a moment while each looked through the pages of the story.

"Maybe the really important part?" Jack suggested.

"Okay. Like when he went out and the other guy found him?" Gayle replied.

"Yeah. He found him, but then did he die?"

"Yeah, I guess he was reaching for him, but then he fell, so the other one got saved."

"So is that the important part, or that the other guy went on and made it to the top?" Jack asked.

"But it said he didn't make it, remember? They asked him and he said no."

"Yeah, but the ax was there so he had to make it," Jack explained.

"Oh, I didn't get that part," Gayle admitted. "So he made it but just said he didn't? Why'd he do that? I'd tell everyone I made it. Yeah, that's probably more important."

"Yeah, but could he have made it if the other guy hadn't saved him?"

"Okay, so maybe they are both important. So we could do a picture of him saving him and then making it, putting the ax on top?" Gayle asked.

"Uh, well, maybe, but the picture is like a symbol."

"Yeah."

"You know how if he hadn't saved him then he wouldn't have made it to the top? Well, you know how those two things are like tied together? Then maybe this is how becoming the top man wouldn't have happened without some other things happening. So like hooks hooked together?" Jack suggested.

"Uh, maybe." Silence for a moment, then Gayle continued. "Maybe instead of hooks, draw a mountain and a chain going around it, and on different parts of the chain we could put him falling, and then put the ax, and then put the other one sitting at the top of the mountain. Like to show they are all connected."

"That's good," Jack said, nodding and reaching for the paper.

Across the room, another pair of students discussed their sketches.

"So that's it? Just a question mark?" Belinda asked.

"Yeah, if that's really the question, you know, who the top man is."

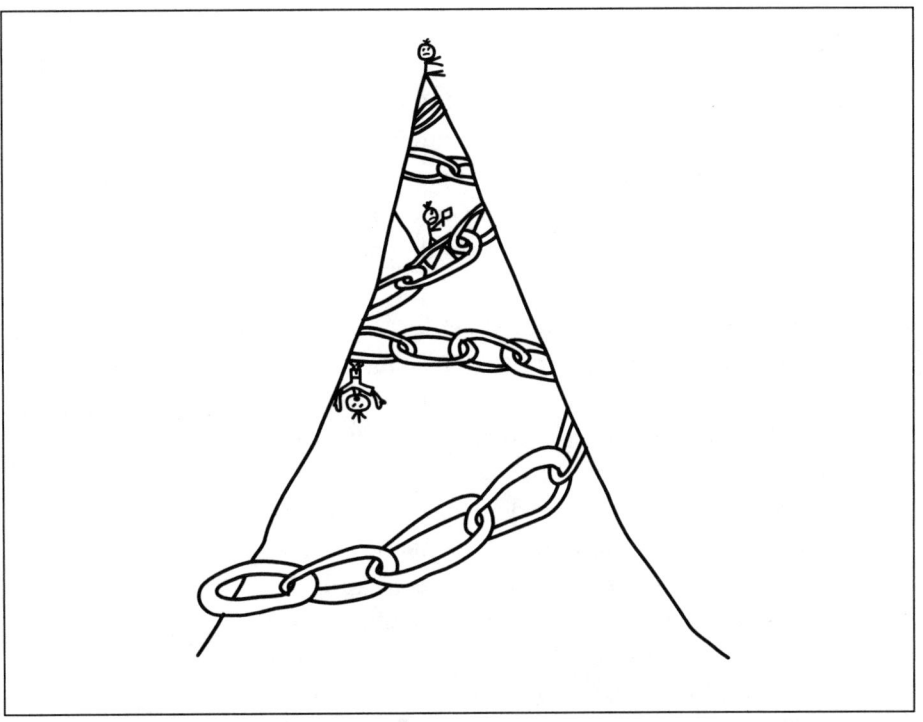

"Well, I think the top man is the one that died, because he saved his friend; so I don't want a question mark," Belinda said.

SKETCH TO STRETCH STRATEGY

"Yeah, okay, but I think the other one who went up to the top and put his ax there and then said he didn't make it is the top man. That was showing how he cared more about his friend than himself," Sarah argued.

"It's like there are two top men," Belinda said.

"So, that's why I thought a question mark: It's like you don't really know."

"No, it's more that you have to decide than that you don't know," Belinda countered.

By the end of the twenty-five minutes, all the students had finished their discussions and most were putting finishing touches on their drawings. The teacher put the students into larger groups (about six students) to share their sketches. After students showed their sketches without making comments, other students in the group said what they thought the sketches symbolized; then the artists explained what they meant to them. By the end of the class, students had seen the effectiveness of Sketch to Stretch.

What's Going On?

As students in Ms. Garza's class were deciding on their sketches, they were discussing main ideas, identifying cause-and-effect relationships, making inferences, and drawing conclusions. Jack's idea of drawing hooks to show how events in the story are connected indicates that he was thinking about cause-and-effect relationships. Belinda and Sarah were drawing conclusions as they politely argued about who the top man is.

That happens often as students use this strategy. As students think of ideas for their sketches, they find themselves rereading the text, thinking about events in the story and what caused them, and drawing conclusions. That is because the strategy requires them to draw a symbolic picture. If students were simply asked to illustrate a scene, they'd be reading for literal information; however, when asked to draw symbolically, they have to think at a more abstract level. As a result, students begin to make inferences and generalizations.

Sketch to Stretch, like any strategy, is a means of getting students to use critical-thinking skills while they read. We want students to recognize cause-and-effect relationships, identify the main idea, make inferences, draw conclusions, and form generalizations. This strategy encourages students to think in these ways. The more they use these skills, the more automatic critical thinking becomes. Eventually, Sketch to Stretch isn't needed as a way to encourage good reading and can instead be used simply as a springboard to discussion. For either purpose, the strategy encourages closer examination of the text and what it means to the reader.

> *Sketch to Stretch encourages closer examination of the text and what it means to the reader.*

SKETCH TO STRETCH STRATEGY

Getting the Strategy to Work

- **Introduce the strategy to students.** Begin, as Ms. Garza did, by showing students some symbolic pictures from a text. Until you've got a group of pictures former students have made based on texts your class is familiar with, you'll need to create some. As you discuss the pictures, make sure students understand that the drawings are symbolic representations of what the story means to them and not literal illustrations of events from the story.

- **Then, have students create their sketches.** After students have read a selection, let them work alone or with a partner to create a sketch. If working with a partner, students can discuss their interpretations of the text and either arrive at a consensus about what to draw or draw individual sketches. When they have finished their sketches, have students write on the back of the drawings their explanations of why they drew what they did. Encourage students to use evidence from the text to support their opinions.

- **Finally, have students share their sketches.** Put students into groups to share their sketches. Remind students to let others respond to the sketch before they explain their drawing. Often a response to a sketch triggers a better discussion than the explanation of the sketch. One of the stretching parts of the strategy (Sketch to *Stretch*) is hearing what others say about the sketch, so as often as possible, put students into groups to share their sketches, listen to what others say, and then share their explanations of their drawings.

A Few Questions...

1. **What about the student who consistently wants to create a literal representation of a scene in the text?**
   This may be an indication that the student can't make the generalizations required to think symbolically or that he or she is still thinking at a concrete operational rather than an abstract reasoning stage. Since you can't force abstract thinking, you'll need to continue to model examples of what symbolic pictures look like. Also, I'd keep that student working with a partner so that a lot of discussion takes place.

2. **Do students ever *not* know what to draw?**
   Absolutely. For some students, making one sketch after reading an entire selection or novel might be overwhelming. To help them move ahead, suggest points throughout the selection or text where they might want to stop and make a sketch. Then, they can choose to expand or work from one of these sketches.

SKETCH TO STRETCH STRATEGY

3. **Why is that helpful? Doesn't that just create more sketches they've got to figure out?**
    With smaller chunks of material, students have less to think about; as a result, finding cause-and-effect relationships, determining the main idea, drawing conclusions, and making generalizations is actually easier.

4. **What if the student says he or she can't draw?**
    That happens often. That's one reason this is called *Sketch* to Stretch: It's a sketch, not a completed piece of art. Because the created sketch is supposed to be symbolic, realistic art is not necessary. Some of the best pictures are done with stick figures and very simplistic drawings. To encourage students who lack artistic talent, avoid showing only well-drawn sketches as models. Instead, choose sketches that are strong symbolically, even though they may be very simplistic.

5. **Does Sketch to Stretch work with all types of texts?**
    Students can create sketches for nonfiction as well as fiction, poems as well as novels, expository writing as well as narrative writing. When using the strategy with nonfiction, students sketch the main idea of the text. For example, after reading the Declaration of Independence, a student might draw a map of England and the American Colonies with a broken chain between them.

6. **Is Sketch to Stretch always a postreading strategy?**
    Not always. It is the most effective as a postreading strategy; however, students can create sketches as they are reading. I've occasionally saved sketches from one year to the next and used sketches of a selection or novel as a way of introducing the text. I'll show the sketch; then we'll talk about what it means to us, read the text, and return to the sketch to offer more responses. In that way, it becomes a prereading strategy.

7. **Should students write about what they've drawn?**
    Yes. Students should include a written explanation at the bottom of their sketches or on the back. This enables them to practice expressing their thoughts in writing and helps me to better understand what their symbolic sketches mean to them.

SKETCH TO STRETCH STRATEGY

References

Harste, Jerome C., and Carolyn L. Burke. 1988. *Creating Classrooms for Authors.* Portsmouth, N.H.: Heinemann Publishers.

Lee, Harper. 1960. *To Kill a Mockingbird.* New York: Lippincott.

Sketch to Stretch at a Glance

- The teacher introduces Sketch to Stretch to students by showing and discussing symbolic pictures based on a text.

- After reading a selection, students work independently or with a partner to create symbolic sketches of their interpretations of the text. On the back of their sketches, students write why they drew what they did, using evidence from the text to support their opinions.

- Students share their sketches in small groups, allowing other students to comment before revealing their explanations of their sketches.

SOMEBODY WANTED BUT SO STRATEGY

"Okay, group. Let's get started," Ms. Stemmons said to her class as she moved to the front of the room. "Let's look at what you read last night." A few students in the back right corner of the room moaned, but everyone else began digging through backpacks, pulling out their literature anthologies. "Who remembers the title?"

"Something about a necklace," one person said.

"Yeah. 'The Necklace,'" another said.

"Okay. Who can give a quick summary?" she asked. Twenty-three heads looked down. Several students began thumbing through the pages of their books. Most just sat very still.

Summarizing a short story or a novel appears to be too overwhelming for many students, who either offer nothing or restate everything in the story. **Somebody Wanted But So**, or **SWBS** (MacOn et al. 1991), offers students a framework to help them create their summaries. Students read a story and then decide who the *Somebody* is, what that somebody *Wanted, But* what happened to keep something from happening, and *So*, finally, how everything worked out.

SWBS also helps students move beyond summary writing. As students choose names for the *Somebody* column, they are deciding which characters are the main characters. In the *Wanted* column, they look at events of the plot and talk about main ideas and details. With the *But* column they are examining conflict. With the *So* column they are identifying the resolution.

SOMEBODY WANTED BUT SO STRATEGY

Step into a Classroom

A Classroom Model

"Anyone?" Ms. Stemmons said. She waited a few more seconds and then wrote four words on the chalkboard like this:

Then she said, "Okay, name a somebody from this story."

"The lady, uh, Loisel," a girl said.

"Right," Ms. Stemmons said, writing that name on the board under the word *Somebody*. "Mrs. Loisel. Who was somebody else?"

"Her husband," another girl said. "Mr. Loisel."

"Good," the teacher said, writing "Mr. Loisel" under "Mrs. Loisel." "Now, who can tell me what Mrs. Loisel wanted?"

"She wanted to be rich," a boy said.

"And she wanted to go to that dance," another student said.

A girl began saying, "Yeah, but she didn't have the right clothes—"

"Wait a second," Ms. Stemmons said, interrupting her. "Don't get ahead of me," she said as she wrote "wanted to be rich" and "wanted to go to the dance" under the *Wanted* column. "Okay, now, Shelly, what did you say?"

SOMEBODY WANTED BUT SO STRATEGY

"But she didn't have the right clothes and jewelry and stuff."

Ms. Stemmons wrote "but she didn't have the right clothes and jewelry."

"I get it," a boy in the front row said. "Put *so she bought a dress and borrowed a necklace* under that last column, that *So* column." Ms. Stemmons did that.

Now the board looked like this:

Somebody	Wanted	But	So
Mrs. Loisel	wanted to be rich and wanted to go to the dance,	but she didn't have the right clothes and jewelry,	so she bought a dress and borrowed a necklace.
Mr. Loisel			

"Is that the whole story?" the teacher asked.

"Wait, don't you think that just saying that she bought the dress isn't enough?" a girl in the middle of the room asked.

"Well, that's what she did," another responded.

"Not really," the girl said. "She made her husband feel guilty, so he gave up his money for her."

"Yeah," several agreed.

One student said to Ms. Stemmons, "Under the *So* column, can you change that to *so she shamed her husband into buying her the dress*?"

"Okay," Ms. Stemmons said and made the change. "Is that the end of the story?" she asked.

"No. She lost the necklace and had to work really hard to pay it back," a student said.

"Yeah, but then she found out that it was like cubic zirconia or something. You know, fake," another said.

"Can you make that fit into the chart?" Ms. Stemmons asked, adding the word *THEN* to the board.

"Okay," one of the boys from the back right corner said. "Mrs. Loisel wanted to give back the necklace after she wore it, but she had lost it, so she and her

SOMEBODY WANTED BUT SO STRATEGY

husband had to find a new one and then borrow money to buy it so she could return the replacement to her friend."

Ms. Stemmons took down what he said, so now the chart looked like this:

Somebody	Wanted	But	So
Mrs. Loisel	wanted to be rich and wanted to go to the dance,	but she didn't have the right clothes and jewelry,	so she shamed her husband into buying her the dress and she borrowed a necklace.
THEN			
Mrs. Loisel	wanted to give back the necklace after she wore it,	but she had lost it,	so she and her husband had to find a new one and then borrow money to buy it so she could return the replacement to her friend.
Mr. Loisel			

"And then what happened?" Ms. Stemmons asked after she had read everything on the chart.

"Put down that they had to take on extra jobs to pay back the borrowed money, and one day ten years later she saw her friend and wanted her friend to know the truth, but her friend told her it was a fake, so she and her husband had done all that work for nothing."

After Ms. Stemmons finished writing that statement, everyone looked at the chart for a moment.

"That's pretty cool," one student said.

SOMEBODY WANTED BUT SO STRATEGY

"Does it work every time?" another asked.

"What about Mr. Loisel? If you started with him would everything change?" another one asked.

"Could you get it down to one statement, you know, with no *thens*?" another wondered.

Ms. Stemmons waited until the comments stopped, then she divided the class into groups of three or four students. She told two of the groups to figure out what the SWBS statement would be for Mr. Loisel. She told two more groups to choose some other stories they had read that year and see if SWBS would work for them. She told the final two groups to see if they could get the SWBS statements that were on the overhead projector down to just one SWBS statement. Students immediately went to work. Here's what three students said while writing a SWBS statement in which Mr. Loisel was the *somebody*.

Erin:	Okay, so we got that Mr. Loisel wanted to make his wife happy, but she constantly wanted what he couldn't afford, so both of them ended up miserable.
Catherine:	This one was like more general than what we did for Mrs. Loisel.
Margaret:	Yeah, this is more of a general summary than a real plot summary like the one on the board. Should we do it like that one?
Erin:	No, I like this one better. This is a better summary of the meaning of the story.
Margaret:	So what would that be for Mrs. Loisel?
Catherine:	Um, Mrs. Loisel wanted people to think she was rich, so she borrowed what she thought was an expensive necklace, but she lost it and had to spend the rest of her life earning money to repay it, so she ended up poorer than when she began.
Erin:	That one still has a lot of the detail. I guess maybe it has to since it is the one that focuses on the main character who was doing everything. Maybe?
Catherine:	Yeah, but Mr. Loisel was important, too. He was important because he was so opposite of her. He wanted to do things to make his wife happy, but she wasn't too worried about making him happy. He must have really loved his wife a lot to put up with how she acted.
Margaret:	He should have told her to repay it herself or to be honest with her friend.
Catherine:	I think he should have told her to grow up. I mean, he gave up that gun he wanted to buy, and he even got her the invitation to begin with. She was just so greedy that she always wanted more.

ELEMENTS OF LITERATURE

SOMEBODY WANTED BUT SO STRATEGY

What's Going On?

Ms. Stemmons' class has given you a glimpse of what an effective strategy Somebody Wanted But So is. Her students, a mixed group of proficient and struggling readers, all enjoyed the strategy and participated in the discussion that ensued after students finished their group work. At first, none of these students wanted to offer a summary of "The Necklace." However, once the framework SWBS was offered, students were not only willing to summarize, but also were interested in the summaries they were creating.

As the girls in Ms. Stemmons' class created the SWBS statement for Mr. Loisel, they noticed that some summaries are detailed and others are general. Plus, through SWBS they began a discussion about character differences and character motivations. This single strategy not only provides a structure for writing summaries, but also helps students to identify main ideas and details, recognize cause-and-effect relationships, make generalizations, identify character differences, and understand how shifting the point of view emphasizes different aspects of the story.

Getting the Strategy to Work

You can either introduce the strategy with a short story, like Ms. Stemmons did, or with a picture book or poem. Generally, students of all levels learn this strategy quickly and are able to use it on their own within a short period of time. SWBS can be used to practice creating and evaluating summaries and to talk about literary elements.

- **To Summarize:** If you want students to work on writing summaries, have them write the words *Somebody Wanted But So* at the top of their own papers and write what they need. Sometimes, as in Ms. Stemmons' classroom, students need to connect several SWBS statements with *and* or *then*. This happens especially if students are reading longer works. When using SWBS with longer works, such as novels, I generally have students write an SWBS statement after every chapter. Then, once the book is finished, students share all their SWBS statements, discuss differences, and, in small groups, see if they can develop an overall SWBS statement for the book. After going through this process for Robert O'Brien's book *Z for Zachariah*, one student wrote in his journal, "Now when I read I constantly see this SWBS pattern. Even long books are just a series of somebody doing something, but then there's a problem that eventually gets solved. I like this a lot." Another student wrote, "When our group had to write an SWBS for *Z for Zachariah* that was just one statement with no *ands* or *thens*, we thought it was impossible. But then we noticed that it was like a different SWBS. It was more about the theme of the

SOMEBODY WANTED BUT SO STRATEGY

book." A third student, one who had told me he would "rather scrape the scum off a bathtub than read a book," wrote, "Now I can write summaries. I never noticed that they had a pattern."

- **To Discuss Literary Elements:** SWBS can also be used to focus on a specific literary element. When discussing conflict, you can ask students to write SWBS statements for two characters from the same story and to tell how the *But* columns differ for the two. You can also have them write two SWBS statements for the same character, one which describes an internal conflict and the other, an external conflict. When talking about point of view, you can ask students to write SWBS statements for two characters from a story and to tell how changing the character changes other aspects of the story.

A Few Questions . . .

1. **SWBS does look simple, but don't students come up with different statements for the same story?**
   Yes, they certainly do, but that's not really a problem. You look at the statements and figure out which students are still at the and-then-this-happened stage (recognizable by many SWBS statements strung together by the word *and*) and which are able to generalize; you quickly see which students do not recognize cause-and-effect relationships; you see which students understand main ideas and which don't; you see which ones can distinguish main ideas from details. You use students' statements to evaluate their progress and to help you decide what you need to teach next.

2. **Since this is a strategy that focuses on summarizing, is it primarily a postreading strategy?**
   Yes, and it's a during-reading strategy if students are writing SWBS statements as they go through a book.

3. **Can this strategy be used for more than teaching how to summarize?**
   Absolutely. As students complete an SWBS chart, they are looking at characters, events, conflicts, and resolutions. They write summaries from different points of view, they evaluate which summaries are the best, and they note how changing the *Somebody* column changes everything else. They have to identify main events, recognize cause-and-effect relationships, and decide which characters are worth discussing. I've even seen teachers use it to encourage students to predict what will happen next. (To use for prediction, simply say to students, "Well, if this is what has happened so far, what do you think so-and-so will want to do next?" or "What will be the next conflict?" or

SOMEBODY WANTED BUT SO STRATEGY

"What will get resolved next?" As students create those statements, they are using prior information from the story to make an educated guess about what will happen next.)

References

O'Brien, Robert. 1975. *Z for Zachariah*. New York: Atheneum.

MacOn, James M., Diane Bewell, and Maryellen Vogt. 1991. *Responses to Literature*. Newark, Del.: International Reading Association.

Somebody Wanted But So at a Glance

- After students read a story, they work alone or in groups to fill in columns on the Somebody Wanted But So chart: who the *Somebody* in a story is, what he or she *Wanted*, *But* what happened that created a problem, and *So* how the problem was resolved. Students join statements with the word *then* when needed.

- Students work together to condense SWBS statements into concise summaries or to develop summaries for long texts such as novels.

- To focus on literary elements, students can write SWBS statements for different characters in the same story or for different types of conflicts.

STORY IMPRESSIONS STRATEGY

We often get impressions about texts before we read them. Tell me a book is by Stephen King, and I form an impression; tell me it is by Flannery O'Connor, and I have another impression. Sometimes those impressions are right and sometimes they are wrong, but they help me begin to think about the text. Impressions, vague and imprecise as they are, help us predict what may happen in the text.

Some readers never form these predictions. They begin reading with no thought of what might happen; therefore, they aren't using their prior experiences to help them understand the text. Predicting, or thinking ahead, is based on the ability to bring previous knowledge to a new situation. If students don't predict, they aren't using what they already know to help them understand what they are about to encounter.

To help readers form predictions about a text, use **Story Impressions** (McGinley and Denner 1987), a strategy that helps students form an overall impression of a text. The teacher gives students ten to fifteen words taken from a text. Keeping these words in the order that the teacher prescribed, students write a brief paragraph that uses each word and summarizes what they think the text will be about. Creating the summary helps students focus on the text and encourages them to start thinking about the key words and concepts the teacher has chosen. Students activate prior knowledge, make predictions, and form a bridge to comprehension.

STORY IMPRESSIONS STRATEGY

Step into a Classroom

A Classroom Model

"Here are your words," the teacher told the twenty-seven students as she flipped on the overhead projector. "No talking. Copy them on your paper and then write your paragraph."

The students sat still. A few had their heads down on their desktops; a few more were sitting sideways in their seats, staring straight ahead with looks of boredom on their faces or looking at the person behind them. A few watched the teacher. All the students read below grade level and had failed the reading portion of the achievement test for several years in a row.

"You'll need paper and a pen, folks," the teacher said. No one moved. "Now," she said slowly. Some stirred.

"What are we gonna do?" one young man asked.

The teacher didn't say anything but instead flipped on the overhead projector.

"Oh, we did this," another student said.

"What?" someone responded.

"You know, those arrows. Remember? The words go together and you figure it out," the student explained.

Several students turned toward the overhead projector and began to read the words. "What's the second one?" one girl called out.

"Gary Paulsen," someone said.

"Who's he?" someone else asked.

"Do you want to work alone or with a partner?" the teacher asked. No one said anything.

"Okay, your choice. If you want to work alone,

true story
↓
Gary Paulsen
↓
trapping animals
↓
sled dogs
↓
watching one dog
↓
learning lessons about animals
↓
quit trapping
↓
sled accident
↓
hurt knee
↓
dogs return
↓
learning more lessons

get started. If you want a partner, grab one person and then get started. But both of you need to write the Story Impression."

Students began getting paper, borrowing pens, and looking around for a partner. Soon, though, the only noise was some whispering as students talked about the words. Here's what Julian and Philip said:

Julian: So you think that Gary Paulsen is trapping animals with his sled dogs?
Philip: What's a sled dog?
Julian: You know, like in the snow, they pull a sled.
Philip: Why would you trap animals in the snow?
Julian: For fur—like trappers?

While Julian and Philip were figuring out what sled dogs and trapping animals might be about, Bonnie and Jessica were having this discussion:

Bonnie: Okay, so it's a true story about Gary Paulsen, and he went out trapping animals on his sled with his sled dogs, and while they were trapping he watched one dog, and that taught him lessons about animals.
Jessica: So you think he learned about the animals he was trapping? You know, like he caught something and saw it didn't like to be trapped?
Bonnie: Yeah, so that would be why he quit trapping.

While those four students worked in pairs, Anne worked alone. Soon she had written the following Story Impression:

> This is a <u>true story</u> about <u>Gary Paulsen</u> when he was <u>trapping animals</u>. He had lots of <u>sled dogs</u>. While <u>watching one dog</u>, he spent lots of his time <u>learning lessons about animals</u>. He got lots of people to <u>quit trapping</u> animals. He was in a <u>sled accident</u> and he had a <u>hurt knee</u>. All of his <u>dogs returned</u> to see how he was. Now he is <u>learning more lessons</u>.

After about twenty minutes, most students had completed the project and gotten together in groups of five or six to read and compare their Story Impressions. Once everyone had shared their impressions, the teacher asked if there was anything that had caused a lot of confusion or had resulted in

STORY IMPRESSIONS STRATEGY

very different responses. One student mentioned that some people in her group thought the animals that Gary Paulsen learned a lesson from were the trapped animals, while others thought that the word *animals* referred to the sled dogs. The teacher just nodded.

When no other comments were offered, she directed them to read an excerpt from Gary Paulsen's autobiography *Woodsong*. "Read it in pairs or to yourself. But as you read, look at how Paulsen connects the words and ask yourself if you did it like he did or differently." Students began reading, and soon there were whispered comments of "Look what he did" and "Oh, we said . . ." and "I like mine better" and even "Oh, I see." The bell rang before the class finished reading the story. The teacher told students to return the next day with the story read and comments about how creating their Story Impressions helped them understand the story.

The next day, Anne said:

> I liked his story better than mine. My impression was kind of different, but because I had those words I knew what to expect. Doing this lets me see what to expect, and then it is like a fun thing to do because I can compare and see if I was correct. When I don't know what to expect, then I have to read slower.

Brandy offered this:

> Sometimes when I do this [write a Story Impression] it makes me read like thinking-reading. I go, "Oh look, he said this," to myself and then it even makes me go back a few sentences to see how he got there. So I think about what I read and what I wrote all at the same time.

What's Going On?

Brandy is correct. Writing a Story Impression does encourage students to think about the text. Students pay more attention to the text as they check to see how their impressions match the author's story.

Although this strategy requires some work from the teacher, the results are worth the work. In the earlier dialogue, Philip begins to create an understanding of sled dogs and trapping. Bonnie's theory about why the author quit trapping reveals her ability to form cause-and-effect relationships. Anne's acknowledgment of the power of predicting ("[the strategy] lets me see what to expect") is important. Once students buy into the worth of a strategy, they are much more likely to use it.

Story Impressions helps readers become engaged with a text before they begin reading. Students discuss what the key words mean and how they could

STORY IMPRESSIONS STRATEGY

be related, explain concepts and terms to one another, and commit their ideas to paper. They make predictions about the text based on what they know about the key words. In addition, students enjoy writing Story Impressions. When you want to encourage students to activate their prior knowledge, make predictions, recognize cause-and-effect relationships, or work on vocabulary, use Story Impressions. The bit of time it takes is well worth the benefits.

> *Story Impressions helps readers become engaged with a text before they begin reading.*

Getting the Strategy to Work

- **First, choose the key words you will use.** After reading the text, choose key words, phrases, or concepts from the story. Your list will normally consist of ten to fifteen words. Give students enough words to form an impression, but not so many that they are able to create the entire story.

- **Next, present the words and discuss their meanings.** Present the words to students in a linked order. The teacher in the dialogue, for example, put the words in a vertical line with arrows connecting one word to the next. It's important for the students to see that the words must be used in a particular order. Then, go through the list, or let students go through the list, to answer any questions about the pronunciation or meaning of the words. This step helps develop students' vocabulary.

- **Have students write and share their summaries.** After discussing the key words and phrases, each student writes a paragraph, using all of the words in their original order, that summarizes what the student thinks the story will be about. Then, students share their Story Impressions and discuss how they linked the key words.

- **Have students read the story and compare it with their Story Impressions.** After students read the story, they will usually want to discuss how their Story Impressions differed from the actual text. Remind students that if their Story Impressions don't match the text, that doesn't mean their predictions were wrong; their predictions just differed from the text.

A Few Questions . . .

1. **Do all Story Impressions need to be written?**
   Yes. Whether it is done independently, with a partner, or in a large group, the Story Impression does need to be written so that students will have something to refer to once they have read the text.

STORY IMPRESSIONS STRATEGY

2. **What if students aren't familiar with the key words I give them?**
   Students become familiar with the key words as they go through the list and discuss their meanings as a class or with a partner. Then, the strategy becomes a vocabulary strategy. The point of Story Impressions is to help students predict how the words could be linked so that they get an impression of the story. Students can't make those links or activate prior knowledge if they don't know what a word or phrase means. Discussing unfamiliar words gives students the opportunity to figure out what they don't know *before* they begin reading.

3. **Doesn't doing Story Impressions give away the ending of the story?**
   It doesn't unless you give so many words in the Story Impression that students are able to recreate the entire story. Make sure you give them only enough words to suggest the main idea. If giving away the ending concerns you, end your list with an earlier event rather than the conclusion of the story.

4. **Isn't this similar to the Probable Passage strategy?**
   Yes. If you haven't looked at that strategy yet, you might want to read about it next (see page 43 in this handbook). Probable Passage is a more structured form of Story Impressions. If you have students who just can't see how key words could be linked together, they may need the structure that Probable Passage provides.

5. **After the students have written their Story Impressions, can they immediately begin reading the story?**
   They can. You'll need to decide how much discussion your students need prior to reading. Some students can take the words home, write their Story Impressions on their own, read the story, and return the next day ready to move on.

6. **What can I expect if students use this strategy?**
   As students think about how key words connect to one another, they are predicting. When they create Story Impressions, they are forming cause-and-effect relationships and making inferences. As they find similarities and differences between their Story Impressions and the text, they are comparing and contrasting.

STORY IMPRESSIONS STRATEGY

References

McGinley, William J., and Peter R. Denner. 1987. Story Impressions: A Prereading/Writing Activity. *Journal of Reading* 31:248–253.

Story Impressions at a Glance

- The teacher chooses key words or phrases from the story students are going to read and arranges them in a linked order.

- The class discusses the words' pronunciations and meanings.

- Using all the key words or phrases in the order they were given, students write brief summaries of what they think the story will be about.

- After reading, students compare their predictions with the actual story.

TEXT REFORMULATION STRATEGY

One night when my daughter was twelve, she handed me her history book, pointed to a particular passage, and said, "I don't get it."

"Don't get what?" I asked.

"It. I don't get it," she replied, thumping the opened page of her book.

I took the book, read the passage, and then put the expository passage into the framework of a narrative example. "Well, Meredith, it's like this. Pretend that . . ." I began.

Ten minutes later she replied, "That is so cool. Why didn't the book just say it that way?"

"What way?" I asked.

"Like that. Like a story. Now it makes sense."

I thought about that exchange for a long time. What had really happened? I asked myself. Eventually, I realized that I had taken a piece of text and transformed it into another type of text. I reformulated the expository text structure to fit the narrative structure Meredith was more familiar with.

Text Reformulation, or Story Recycling (Feathers 1993), is a strategy in which students transform a text into another type of text. Whether students turn expository text into narratives, poems into newspaper articles, or short stories into patterned stories such as ABC books, reformulating texts encourages students to talk about the original texts. In addition, reformulations encourage

TEXT REFORMULATION STRATEGY

students to identify main ideas, cause-and-effect relationships, themes, and main characters while sequencing, generalizing, and making inferences.

Step into a Classroom

A Classroom Model

Seventh period. Late April. Twenty-eight students were all reading Richard Connell's "The Most Dangerous Game." Some were reading in the "Reading Café," a corner of the room with a rocking chair, two beanbag chairs, a small round table with a blue cloth on which sat a lamp, and two wicker chairs with cushions. Some were at the writing station, a table with three word processors, a printer, several thesauruses, and a handbook on usage. Several other students were talking with the teacher. A few were at listening stations wearing headsets and reading along with the cassette tape of "The Most Dangerous Game." The rest were in small groups working on their text reformulations.

Catherine: Okay, read what we've got.

Matt: Okay. *A* is for Africa and Amazon where General Zaroff once killed animals. *B* is for—

John: Wait a sec. I don't think we should say he killed them. He hunted them.

Catherine: Well, what's the difference? If you hunt them, then you kill them.

John: No. That's the point. Look here at this part where he says "I am speaking of hunting." And then Rainsford says, "What you speak of is murder." See, that's the point—that one sees going after men like hunting, and the other like murdering or killing. But both would see hunting animals as okay, so you don't call it killing, you call it hunting. See?

Matt: Okay. So hunted. Now, *B* is for boredom that Zaroff begins to feel. *C* is for—well, we don't have a good *C* yet. *D* is for Death Swamp where Rainsford almost dies. *E* is for the escape that Rainsford must do. *F* is—

John: Wait—I was just thinking for *S*—

Catherine: *S*? We aren't up to *S*.

John: I know, but when Matt said about how Rainsford was trying to escape, I was thinking about how he was in the room at the end, and like how he started to fight, and then he won, and did he really escape?

TEXT REFORMULATION STRATEGY

Matt: You mean, did he get off the island and then come back?

John: No, like did he, did he really . . . Well, S should be for switch because what I'm wondering is, Did he become Zaroff and is he going to just start killing people? So did he escape from Zaroff, or did Zaroff's ways like, you know, turn Rainsford into Zaroff?

Catherine: Oh, I get it. If Rainsford had gotten off the island, then why did he come back?

Matt: Well, he had to come back because he couldn't just keep swimming, but when he came back he had won, and maybe he didn't have to fight with Zaroff. So, yeah, did they switch?

John: Yeah. And so then maybe C could be for confusion?

Catherine: Maybe, but I don't know.

Matt: Well anyway, that's good for S. Now, F is for fear because Rainsford, he felt a fear he had never felt before.

Another group was still trying to decide how to reformulate the text.

Cindy: I think we ought to do the Brown Bear pattern. You know, like "Rainsford, Rainsford, what do you see? I see Zaroff looking at me. Zaroff, Zaroff what do you see? I see Rainsford running from me."

Megan: I don't know. That seems really hard to get everything in. Like the first thing that happened wasn't Rainsford looking at Zaroff.

Cindy: Okay, so we'd just have to start earlier, like "Rainsford, Rainsford, what do you see? I see a black night looking at me."

Megan: Yeah, but then how does the black night see something?

Jennifer: Well, what about "This is the island that Zaroff built. This is the game that Zaroff plays on the island that he built." [*pause*]

Megan: Okay, like "This is Rainsford, the man that Zaroff hunted that is part of the game that Zaroff plays on the island that he built."

Cindy: Yeah. But you don't say how Rainsford got there.

Megan: You could say, "This is the way that Rainsford fell off the ship in the middle of the night and the game that he plays on his island that he built."

Cindy: This is going to get really long.

Megan: Well, not if we pick like the really important parts.

Jennifer: Okay, that's what we need to do. So what is like important?

Cindy: Like falling off the ship . . .

Both groups worked all period and part of the next day completing their reformulations.

TEXT REFORMULATION STRATEGY

What's Going On?

In the previous dialogue, students in both groups used reading skills such as sequencing (Cindy's comment that "we'd just have to start earlier"), identifying main ideas (Group Two's discussion of the "really important parts"), and making inferences (John's explanation of the word *switch*). As the students worked through their reformulations, they returned to the text, reread portions, argued over meanings, decided whether something was important or not, and listened to each other's interpretations.

Getting students to think about the text is always the goal. Text reformulation encourages students to think critically about the text without overwhelming them. The teacher never has to tell students to "find the main idea" or "make an inference"; they use these skills naturally while working on their reformulations. As students begin the process of reformulating, they must analyze and evaluate not only the text but also the writing they are creating about the text.

> *Text Reformulation encourages students to think critically about the text without overwhelming them.*

Additionally, they must use these skills as they ask themselves how best to reformulate a particular text. Eventually, students begin to see how form influences the message. After doing several reformulations, one student said, "This story had to be done like an ABC book because it was true, and that's what ABC books are—just telling you something, like A is for apple. And because everything happened in this story bam, bam, bam—just one thing after another. That's what happens when you read an ABC book; you just turn those pages one right after another."

Getting the Strategy to Work

- **First, introduce the strategy.** When you introduce students to this strategy, they usually do better if you have them reformulate the text into some sort of patterned structure. (Examples of how to model this strategy using patterned texts are found in the MiniRead Skill Lessons and Selection Skill Lessons section of the *Reading Skills and Strategies* binder.) There are several types of patterned structures that students can use:

  1. **Fortunately/Unfortunately structure:** "Fortunately I set my alarm clock last night. Unfortunately I forgot to turn it on. Fortunately my little brother woke me. Unfortunately he used his new water pistol...."

  2. **If/Then structure:** "If the dog chases the cat, the cat will run up a tree. If the cat gets stuck in the tree, you'll have to get her down...."

TEXT REFORMULATION STRATEGY

For other examples of the If/Then structure, see *If You Give a Mouse a Cookie* and other books by Laura Joffe Numeroff.

3. **Cumulative tale structure:** (like *The House That Jack Built* or *The Twelve Days of Christmas*)

4. **ABC book structure:** "A is for _____. B is for _____. . . ."

5. **Repetitive book structure:** *Brown Bear, Brown Bear, What Do You See?* by Bill Martin, Jr.

- **Model several types of reformulations.** Some students choose always to do patterned-text reformulations; other students, though, begin to explore various types of reformulations. Students might try the following reformulations:
  — short stories into comic books, letters, or interviews
  — poems into stories or letters
  — stories into plays, radio announcements, newspaper ads, or television commercials
  — plays into poems or newspaper stories
  — nonfiction (like history or science books) into stories
  — diaries or memoirs into plays, newspaper articles, or television news-magazine scripts

- **Decide whether you or the students will choose the type of reformulation.** You can tell students what type of reformulation to use; however, I wouldn't suggest doing that all the time. Part of the benefit of the strategy results from students deciding exactly what type of reformulation works best. Sometimes, though, you might want students to work on cause-and-effect relationships; in that case, ask them to reformulate using the Fortunately/Unfortunately or If/Then pattern. Sometimes you might want them to look at characterization; in that case, suggest that they reformulate the text into an interview. If you want students to practice writing summaries, have them recycle the story into a movie preview.

- **Provide opportunities for practice and evaluation.** Text Reformulation must be used repeatedly for students to realize its full benefits. These reformulations can be used to evaluate students' progress. Make sure, however, that you don't penalize students for something they've omitted in their reformulation if you didn't tell them to include it. If you want to see whether they are identifying cause-and-effect relationships, tell them to make sure that is apparent in what they write.

> *Text Reformulation must be used repeatedly for students to realize its full benefits.*

ELEMENTS OF LITERATURE

TEXT REFORMULATION STRATEGY

A Few Questions...

1. **How often should students reformulate a text?**
   I can think of nothing worse than knowing that every time I read something I am going to have to rewrite it into some other form, so every time is too often. On the other hand, twice during the school year is too seldom. I suggest that you don't think in terms of a number, but instead, introduce the strategy, model it several times using several different types of reformulations, and then make it one way for students to demonstrate that they can identify main ideas, sequence events, generalize, infer, analyze, and synthesize.

2. **Can I tell whether students have used those skills just by reading their reformulations?**
   Probably. If the reformulation puts events in the selection out of sequence, then you'll know that sequencing didn't occur. However, sometimes the reformulation will not include an example of a particular skill, such as making an inference. Does that mean the students can't infer? No, all that means is that the reformulation doesn't show you that skill.

3. **What about students who hate to write? Won't they hate this strategy?**
   That's a great question because struggling readers often don't like to write. There are several things to consider when you tell these students to do something that requires writing. First, when students say they don't like to write, often they mean exactly that—they don't like to put pen to paper. It rarely means that they don't like to make up stories. To help these students, give them alternatives to writing the story. For instance, perhaps students could record their text reformulation rather than write it. If students are working in groups, the student who doesn't mind writing could be the scribe, or students could take turns writing. Second, sometimes students who don't like to write have trouble deciding how to say what they want to say. The patterned texts offer these students a framework that relieves them of worrying about form. Third, keep text reformulations an option: Optional activities are generally received more favorably than required activities.

References

Feathers, Karen. 1993. *InfoText*. Portsmouth, N.H.: Heinemann Publishers.
Numeroff, Laura J. 1985. *If You Give a Mouse a Cookie*. New York: Harper Collins.
Martin, Bill, Jr. 1983. *Brown Bear, Brown Bear, What Do You See?* New York: Holt, Rinehart and Winston.

TEXT REFORMULATION STRATEGY

Text Reformulation at a Glance

- The teacher introduces Text Reformulation by having students reformulate a text they have read into a patterned story, such as an If/Then or ABC story.

- The teacher models several types of reformulations.

- Either the teacher or the students choose which type of reformulation to do based on the desired learning objective.

THINK-ALOUD STRATEGY

It happens all the time. You ask students to tell you something about what they've read, and they meet your request with blank stares. They seem to know nothing about the text, but they maintain they've read it. Many of these students have done what they consider reading: Their eyes have traveled over the words from left to right and from top to bottom, and they've turned pages at the appropriate time. What they haven't done is pay any attention to what those words mean; they haven't been thinking about what they are reading. That's when a strategy called Think-Aloud can help.

The **Think-Aloud** strategy (Davey 1983; Olshavsky 1976–77) helps readers think about how they make meaning. As students read, they pause occasionally to think aloud about connections they are making, images they are creating, problems with understanding that they are encountering, and ways they see of fixing those problems. This oral thinking not only helps the teacher understand why or how a student is having difficulty with a text, but also encourages the student to think about the text while reading it. Students learn to think about their reading and to monitor their understanding.

Step into a Classroom

A Classroom Model

I sat in the high school reading lab with Bonnie for about fifteen minutes, listening to her read aloud *A Christmas Carol*. Bonnie's teacher had asked me to work with her because she was having problems understanding what she

THINK-ALOUD STRATEGY

read. When she finished a section and I asked her to tell me what had happened, she either stared blankly at the wall, met my eyes briefly before shrugging and looking away, or looked back quickly at the text before shaking her head. The next day, I met her in the lab again and gave her a Think-Aloud bookmark.

Identifying problems	**F**ixing problems	
	Picturing the text	**P**redicting what happens next
		Making comparisons **M**aking comments

"What's this?" she asked, turning the laminated bookmark over.

"It's a Think-Aloud bookmark. Use it while you read to help you keep on the right line and to suggest the kinds of things you should be thinking while you are reading. While you read, you ask yourself questions, make predictions, make connections, make comments, or fix problems you're having," I said, pointing out those terms on the bookmark.

"How?" Bonnie replied.

"Like this," I said and began to model how to do a Think-Aloud by reading a portion of *A Christmas Carol*. (The quotation marks indicate what I read from the text. My Think-Aloud comments are in brackets.)

> Here I've identified a problem and offered one way to fix that problem.

"This lunatic, in letting Scrooge's nephew out, had let two other people in." [Well, here's a problem. I don't remember who was doing what yesterday, so I don't know who the lunatic is. I guess I could go back, but I think I'll just go on and see if I start remembering.] "They were portly gentlemen, pleasant to behold . . ." [That's confusing. *A port is a place where boats dock, and it is also a kind of wine, so I can't picture what portly gentlemen are. But it can't be something bad because it says they were pleasant. Hmm.]* ". . . and now stood, with their hats off, in Scrooge's office. They had books and papers in their hands, and bowed to him." [Why are they bowing? Maybe this is set in the last century when people used to bow all the time. I keep seeing these three men all standing around bowing to each other over and over again like in some comedy movie, but I get the idea that they aren't going to be funny.] "'Scrooge and Marley's, I believe,' said one of the gentlemen, referring to his list." [What list? I don't get it. Did we read about a list yesterday? I'm afraid I might have to back up and do some rereading because I'm confused. Or maybe I'm not supposed to know what the list is, and perhaps Scrooge doesn't know either. Maybe his figuring it out becomes important.]

> I'm identifying another problem and also picturing the text.

> Now, I've not only questioned the text, but I am also picturing the action and making a prediction.

> Here I've combined a question with a prediction.

116 Reading Strategies Handbook THINK-ALOUD

THINK-ALOUD STRATEGY

At this point, Bonnie interrupted me and said, "What are you doing? You are reading, but then you keep talking."

"I'm just saying aloud the kinds of things I think about when I'm reading. That way you can hear what I'm thinking."

"You mean you think that stuff when you are reading?"

"Sure. That's how I figure out what's going on. I had a lot of questions, and I also was predicting what I thought might happen. I could have done some other kinds of thinking, like making a comment or connecting something in the story to something else, but I just wasn't having those thoughts. Don't you do that when you read?" I asked.

"No."

"You should. Thinking about what you are reading will help you understand it better. Here, you try. Read aloud, and when you come to a part that reminds you of something else, that puzzles you, that you want to comment on, or that gives you an idea about what might happen next, then say it out loud."

Bonnie began:

> *Here Bonnie pauses to identify a problem by asking a question.*

"'Have I the pleasure of addressing Mr. Scrooge, or Mr. Marley?' *[What does he mean,* addressing? *He isn't writing a letter, is he? Is he talking to him? And who is Marley?]* "'Mr. Marley has been dead these seven years,' Scrooge replied." *[Okay, so they are talking. But what does he mean by "these" seven years? What other seven years could it be?]* "'He died seven years ago, this very night.'" *[Oh, that's weird, and now these guys show up looking for him? Maybe they think that Scrooge killed him and they think he is going to do something on the same day of his killing, and so they are there to keep him from doing that.]* "'We have no doubt his liberty is well represented by his surviving partner,' said the gentleman, presenting his credentials." *[I don't get it. None of this makes any sense.]*

> *Bonnie begins by making a comment and goes on to make a prediction.*

> *Now she fixes up one of her problems and asks more questions.*

> *Bonnie stops at this point, frustrated, as she identifies a problem.*

Before Bonnie and I began talking about the text, we talked about her Think-Aloud. "I hated it," Bonnie declared. "It made reading this really slow, and look how dumb I sounded. All it did was point out everything I didn't know."

"When you read yesterday, did you know what kinds of things you didn't know," I asked, "or were you unsure what parts were confusing you?"

"I guess I just read it and that was all," she admitted.

"Just now, when you did the Think-Aloud, you sounded like you could figure out what was hard." I showed her the tally I had been keeping of her comments. "Look, you made a prediction, asked some questions, fixed up a problem, and made a comment."

"But it didn't make me understand it any better."

ELEMENTS OF LITERATURE   Reading Strategies Handbook   117

THINK-ALOUD STRATEGY

"Sure it did," I reassured her. "You can't figure out something if you don't know what parts you don't understand."

Bonnie and I met three days a week for thirty minutes over the next three months. The regular practice with Think-Alouds improved her comprehension and fluency. After about six weeks, she had started reading longer sections before pausing to think aloud. Here's a portion of a Think-Aloud that Bonnie did with Cynthia Voigt's novel *Dicey's Song*. Bonnie's comments are in brackets.

After reading a paragraph about a character sketch that Dicey's teacher wanted Dicey to write, Bonnie paused. *[So what's a character sketch? Is she supposed to be reading a book and drawing a character?]* She continued reading and discovered that Dicey could think of lots of people to write about. Then Bonnie paused again. *[Oh, I get it, like a description paper. That's what we call them. Descriptions. This is like what we had to do last year when we chose somebody and explained what made them the way they were.]* Bonnie continued reading through one page, turned to the next, and paused again after reading a section in which Dicey, while talking with a friend, called the assignment an essay. *[Oh look. Here, she's calling it an essay. Earlier I didn't know what it was, but I figured it out from what she was saying. Here, she just says it differently. So I had a problem and I thought I fixed it, but even if I hadn't, I would have gotten it here.]*

"What if you hadn't been doing the Think-Aloud?" I asked. "Do you still think you would have figured out that *character sketch* and *essay* were the same thing?"

"I guess not. I still don't like these Think-Alouds too much, but you're right—if you think about what you are reading, then you can figure some stuff out. Maybe Think-Alouds are like vegetables—you know that even if you don't like them, they're still good for you."

What's Going On?

A dialogue with the text is something that good readers have constantly as they read, although they usually do it silently. Think-Alouds provide a structure for struggling readers to have a dialogue with a text; they learn to think about their reading and to monitor what they do and do not understand.

> *Think-Alouds provide a structure for struggling readers to have a dialogue with a text.*

118 Reading Strategies Handbook

THINK-ALOUD

THINK-ALOUD STRATEGY

When students Think-Aloud, they can do several things. They can

- **predict** ("I bet that when she gets home she'll be in trouble.")

- **picture the text** ("From this part here, I can see . . .")

- **make comparisons** ("This reminds me of earlier when she said that she didn't want to be friends" or "This is like how I felt when we moved.")

- **identify comprehension problems** ("I don't get this. What does this mean?" or "What's this about?")

- **fix up those problems** ("Oh, I get it" or "Maybe that part meant . . .")

- **make comments** ("I like this" or "This is pretty gross.")

Any of these comments indicate that the student is actively engaged with the reading. That's the goal. As students use this strategy more and more, thinking about the text becomes more natural, more reflexive. Eventually you want the student to be able to think silently while reading, but don't expect that shift to happen quickly.

Getting the Strategy to Work

- **First, model Think-Alouds.** (For an example of how to model a Think-Aloud, see the skill lesson section of the *Reading Skills and Strategies* binder.) This is truly a strategy that isn't just taught, but is shown—again and again. This strategy can be modeled using a variety of materials. One way is to bring in a difficult text—such as a college chemistry book—and read a passage from that. Then, students can see you really trying to think through a text. Poetry, newspaper articles, sports reports, and graphs all work well as texts for Think-Alouds. When you're modeling, read the first few paragraphs of a selection, pausing to make Think-Aloud comments as you go. Give students a tally sheet (see the Think-Aloud tally sheet on page 124) and let them tally the types of Think-Aloud comments you make. Students might disagree about whether a remark is a comparison or a comment or whether you're visualizing or predicting. That's okay. The point isn't to guess correctly, but to think! This modeling process should take only five to ten minutes of class time.

- **After you've modeled a few, have students Think-Aloud a portion of text with a partner.** The partner's job is to use the tally sheet to record what type of comments the student is making.

- **Provide ample opportunities for students to practice Think-Alouds.** When you first introduce the strategy, model the strategy several days in a row; then, the

THINK-ALOUD STRATEGY

next week, model it several more days in a row. Talk a lot about what you are doing and what kinds of comments you are making. Then, let students try a Think-Aloud with a very short text, such as a poem they've not read before, a MiniRead supplied in this binder, or a passage from their science or history textbooks. Let them practice a couple of days a week for two or three weeks. Then, begin using the strategy with the selections in *Elements of Literature*. Think-Aloud is a strategy students should internalize and use as needed; therefore, you need to remind them frequently to use the strategy. During silent reading time, a student might need to move to a corner of a room to think aloud. Students can't go from seeing you model the strategy to using it when needed without the intermediate step of practice. For a while (several months), build in some class time once a week or once every seven to eight class days for students to think aloud with a partner, into a tape recorder, or with you.

- **Listen to students' Think-Alouds and provide feedback.** Keep in mind that you need to hear some of the Think-Alouds from students. Either schedule a time for students to read and Think-Aloud to you, or set up a listening/recording center where students record their Think-Alouds on a tape. You are listening to hear what types of comments students are making over time. As you listen to students think through a text, you are able to hear problems they are having, how they fix those problems, how well they picture the text, and whether they ever make predictions or connections. Think-Aloud offers you a glimpse into each student's comprehension process.

> *Think-Aloud offers you a glimpse into each student's comprehension process.*

A Few Questions . . .

1. **What should I do if students make Think-Aloud comments for every sentence?**
First, look at your modeling. Are you making Think-Aloud comments after every sentence? If you are, stop! Make a comment as needed. Sometimes that might be after every one or two sentences. Usually you'll go four or five sentences before making a comment. Second, don't worry too much. Many times when students first begin using this strategy, they'll make comments after every sentence. This may be because they are trying to get lots of tally marks on the Think-Aloud tally sheet, because the strategy is something new, or because they are avoiding reading. To help students move past this stage, give them frequent opportunities to use the strategy so the newness wears off. When you aren't listening to one student's Think-Aloud, be sure to circulate

THINK-ALOUD STRATEGY

through the room. If you hear someone pausing at every sentence with comments that don't indicate deep thinking ("I like this"), tell that student to read until he or she has a connection to make, a prediction to offer, or a comment to make about a problem in comprehension.

2. Is it helpful to tell students what kind of Think-Aloud comments to make?

No. While you want to encourage students to move past one type of comment if it is all you hear consistently, telling them to make three of this and four of that type of comment will ensure that they stop thinking about the text and just think about their comments. You should model lots of different types of comments and challenge students to find passages in the text that suggest those types of comments. If students never hear you make a prediction or fix a problem, they won't know how to do it.

3. What if students' Think-Aloud comments are questions they have about the text? Should I answer their questions?

Not as the Think-Aloud is in progress. Often, confusion about what is going on in the text—whether it is wondering what a specific word means, which character is speaking, or what is happening next—is cleared up as the student continues reading. That's when you'll hear comments like "Oh, I get it" or "I bet that part meant . . ." or "That must have been this character who said . . ." When students are finished, however, I think it's a good idea to ask them what questions they still have about the text. These questions can be discussed in a small group, with another reader, or with you.

4. How often and for how long should students practice Think-Alouds?

Think of Think-Alouds as being like any exercise routine. Exercising once every three weeks probably won't give us the results we're after; nor will exercising seven days one week and none the next. Your goal might be to have students do a Think-Aloud once a week. Remember, this isn't a fifty-five-minute ordeal. It's a five- to ten-minute exercise.

A Think-Aloud isn't a fifty-five-minute ordeal. It's a five- to ten-minute exercise.

5. Isn't Think-Aloud similar to the Say Something strategy?

While both Think-Aloud and Say Something (see page 65 in this handbook) are metacognitive strategies that help students think about what they are reading, they are used in different ways. Think-Aloud is done independently; the partner tallies responses but does not participate in the Think-Aloud. Say Something, on the other hand, involves interaction with a partner as students carry on a dialogue about the text.

ELEMENTS OF LITERATURE   Reading Strategies Handbook **121**

THINK-ALOUD STRATEGY

6. **Should students write down the comments that their partners make?**
   They certainly don't have to. Some students write quickly, take good notes, and can listen while they write. They might enjoy jotting down the actual statements that students make while thinking aloud. I wouldn't require it because that might cause some students to constantly tell the reader to slow down, repeat the comment, or ask how to spell something! That's not the point at all.

7. **How do I grade Think-Alouds?**
   To help those students who constantly ask "Is this for a grade?" you can give participation grades. I also use the following evaluation form:

Name _____ Date _____

Text for Think-Aloud

Student completes this portion:

1. The type of comment I made the most often was _____.
   I made this the most often because _____.

2. The type of comment I made the least often was _____.
   I didn't make this very often because _____.

3. A type of comment I would like to make more is _____.

4. Using Think-Aloud with this selection helped me because _____.

To be completed by the teacher:

1. Student's strengths during this Think-Aloud:

2. An area for improvement for the next Think-Aloud:

3. Type of comment the student seems most comfortable making:

4. Type of comment the student might be encouraged to make during the next Think-Aloud:

THINK-ALOUD STRATEGY

After students have used the evaluation form for a while, they begin to see that Think-Alouds help them understand what they are reading.

8. What changes can I expect to see in my students' reading?

Students who are taught the Think-Aloud strategy, who have the opportunity to practice it on a regular basis, who receive feedback about the types of comments they are making, and who keep track of their comments over time, eventually begin doing what we want them to do with texts: thinking about them. When students read actively, question what they are not understanding, make predictions and connections, and visualize what is going on, then they have a better understanding of what they're reading.

References

Davey, Beth. 1983. Think-Aloud: Modeling the Cognitive Processes of Reading Comprehension. *Journal of Reading* 27:44–47.

Olshavsky, Jill Edwards. 1976–77. Reading as Problem-Solving: An Investigation of Strategies. *Reading Research Quarterly* 12:654–674.

Voigt, Cynthia. 1982. *Dicey's Song*. Riverside, N.J.: Atheneum.

Think-Aloud at a Glance

- The teacher models a Think-Aloud for students, letting them tally on the Think-Aloud tally sheet the types of comments the teacher makes (predicting, picturing the text, comparing, commenting, identifying a problem, or fixing up a problem).

- Students practice the strategy with a partner using short and easy texts before using Think-Aloud with their assignments.

- Students regularly practice Think-Alouds, eventually using them on their own as needed.

THINK-ALOUD STRATEGY

Think-Aloud Tally Sheet   Listener:_____

Think-Aloud Comments	Tally
Predicting what happens next	
Picturing the text	
Making comparisons	
Identifying problems	
Fixing problems	
Making comments	

VOCABULARY DEVELOPMENT STRATEGIES

"What's this word?" Martin asked his teacher as he pointed to a word in the book he was reading.

"Agitated," she replied. "Do you know what it means?"

"No—I never heard it before," he replied.

While there's nothing remarkable about Martin's question, his response does offer us a lot of insight. When students have a limited listening vocabulary, they generally have a limited reading vocabulary. That link between listening comprehension and reading comprehension was firmly established in the landmark report *Becoming a Nation of Readers* (CSR 1984), which explains that "the single best predictor of success in reading is the amount of time a child was read aloud to." Struggling and reluctant readers often haven't had the read-aloud experience of avid readers and certainly don't have the independent reading experience of those students. As a result, many of these readers know far fewer words than their avid-reader counterparts.

As these students sit in our classrooms confronted with words they have never heard, we must find ways to increase their vocabularies. Reading aloud to students remains the single best way to improve their vocabularies. It is difficult, however, to read aloud enough to help a secondary student catch up to the student who has been read aloud to consistently since birth. Therefore, other strategies must be used. Strategies such as Words Across Contexts,

VOCABULARY DEVELOPMENT STRATEGIES

Context Clues, and Vocabulary Trees help students learn about words and make the words a part of their own vocabulary.

The **Words Across Contexts** strategy allows students to see how the same word means different things in different contexts. **Context Clues** helps students identify which parts of a sentence or passage will help them understand the unknown word. **Vocabulary Trees** (Hill 1998) helps students learn common Latin and Greek roots and see how those roots become parts of many words.

Step into a Classroom

A Classroom Model

The first-period English class had been underway for about ten minutes when I arrived. All twenty-three students were reading a selection in their literature anthologies, and their teacher, Mr. Franklin, was standing at the back of the room.

"What's up?" I asked him.

"On Thursdays I always give them about thirty-five minutes to read something we are working on in class," he explained.

"Like free reading?" I asked.

"Well, sort of, but not really. It's not completely free because they can't read whatever they want. They can only read what we are working on, unless they are all caught up; then they can read whatever they want. These kids are so busy after school that even if they wanted to read the assignments, sometimes they just don't have the time. So I build in some time. Also, while they are reading in class, they'll sometimes ask me questions about what they are reading that would never get asked if they were only reading at home."

While we were talking, Laticia came up to Mr. Franklin. "Mr. Franklin, look here. It says she 'drove the ball,' and at first I was thinkin' she drove the ball, you know, like drove a car, but it can't be; it has to be somethin' else. And so I was thinkin', What else could *drove* be for? and I think it could be on the Words Across Contexts list. Like 'What could drove mean to a . . . ?' and you could say 'to a car driver,' and then you could say 'to a golfer,' because I heard someone say Tiger Woods drove the ball far. Cool, huh?"

"What was that all about?" I asked as Laticia returned to her desk.

"Well," said Mr. Franklin, "every day when the students come in we discuss how words mean different things in different contexts. For instance, *tackle* means one thing to a football player and another thing to someone

VOCABULARY DEVELOPMENT STRATEGIES

who's going fishing. And *charge* means one thing to an electrician, another thing to a shopper, and another to a soldier. Each day I put up a transparency that has words used in different contexts (see example). I give students one bonus point on a test for each word they can add to our list of words that have different meanings across different contexts. That's what Laticia has done—found a word that she realized could mean something else in another context."

About this time, I saw one student take out his notebook and write something on what looked like a sketch of a tree.

"Lemme see, man," another student whispered loudly to him.

"No way. You get your own," the first whispered back.

"What are they talking about?" I asked Mr. Franklin.

"Those are our vocabulary trees," he said, reaching for a transparency (see example on page 128). "Students write a root or affix in the root section of the tree, put the key word they need to know (usually a word I take from something they are reading) in the trunk part of the tree, and then, in the branches, write other words that contain that root or affix. They try to fill in three smaller twigs from that branch—one twig that says where they've heard the word, one where they've seen it, and one where they themselves have written it. They keep working on their trees all grading period. The more words they have on their trees at the end of the nine weeks, the better their grades."

> *"Tackle means one thing to a football player and another thing to someone who's going fishing."*

Words Across Contexts

What would the word *volume* mean to a musician?
a librarian?

What would the word *ball* mean to Cinderella?
Nolan Ryan?
Clyde Drexler?

What would the word *jersey* mean to
a dairy farmer?
someone from New England?
a seamstress?
a football player?

What would the word *conductor* mean to
an orchestra?
an electrician?
someone on a train?

ELEMENTS OF LITERATURE

VOCABULARY DEVELOPMENT STRATEGIES

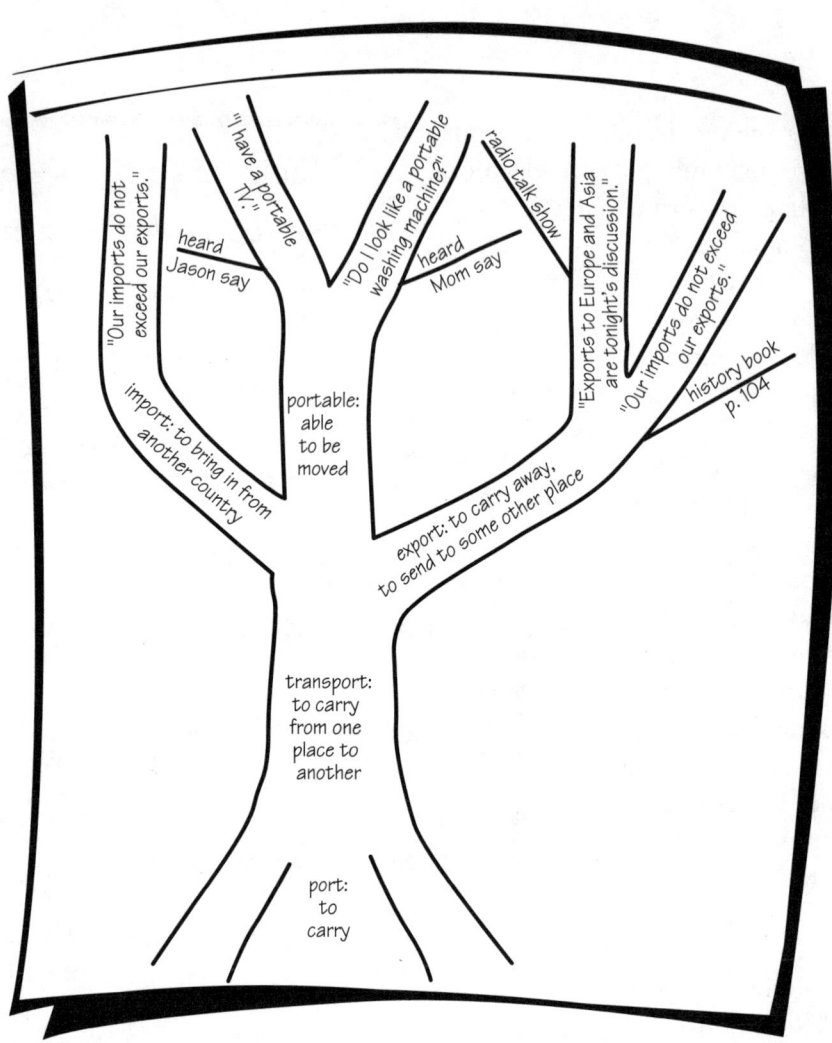

About this time two students came up. "Mr. Franklin, is this a context clue?" one asked, pointing at a sentence that said, "She wondered briefly if her instinct was right. Was that little voice in her head giving her the right information?"

"See that part there?" one of the girls said. "That part that says the 'little voice in her head,' well, isn't that a restatement context clue?"

"Why do you think it might be a restatement?" Mr. Franklin asked.

"'Cause look, it says 'instinct,' and then if you keep on reading, it says 'little voice,' and I think it is like the author telling you that instinct is a little voice, so that makes it a restatement," the second girl explained.

After the two girls had gone back to their desks, Mr. Franklin turned to me and explained, "I was constantly telling students to use context clues, but it didn't seem to be doing any good, so one day I taught them how to recognize context clues. See that poster up there with the clues listed (see example on page 129)? Now I've got students constantly looking at words and the words around words and thinking about the relationships among words. And it works."

VOCABULARY DEVELOPMENT STRATEGIES

> **Types of Context Clues**
>
> 1. **Definition/Explanation:** The author actually defines the word or explains it in the same sentence in which the word appears.
>
> 2. **Restatement/Synonym:** The author restates the meaning of the word or uses a synonym. Restatement/Synonym clues often use signal words.
>
> 3. **Contrast/Antonym:** The author explains the meaning of the word by providing you with an antonym. Contrast/Antonym clues often use signal words.
>
> 4. **Inference/General Context:** The author expects you to infer what the word means by deciding how it is related to other information in the text.

What's Going On?

These students were using three vocabulary strategies—Words Across Contexts, Context Clues, and Vocabulary Trees—to increase their knowledge of words. What's important to note is that students used each strategy on their own. Mr. Franklin didn't have everyone doing the same activity; actually, the students weren't even supposed to be doing anything other than reading. In spite of that, students all focused on words in different ways.

That's what is critical with vocabulary development—giving students multiple ways to expand their understanding of words. Just as one size rarely fits all, one type of vocabulary development rarely works for all students. Mr. Franklin explained that early in the year he had spent a lot of time explaining the strategies his students were using. Now, several months into school, that time was paying off as students, on their own, were beginning to look at words.

Getting the Strategies to Work

Words Across Contexts is an important strategy because it takes words that students already know and shows them how to use those words in other situations. It gets them on the road to thinking about words and how words are used—something that many readers resist. I've often started the first day of

VOCABULARY DEVELOPMENT STRATEGIES

school with this strategy. On the first day, every student makes a small banner and writes the following title across the top: "(Student's name) is an expert at (name of activity)." Some students say they are experts at watching television; others mention a sport or subject area. In a column below this statement, they list ten words related to the activity (see example). For the first few days, students discuss one of the Words Across Contexts questions (see page 127) that is on a transparency on the overhead projector when they enter the room.

After the fourth day, when all the students have finished their banners, they look for words on the banners that can mean different things in different contexts. For instance, the word *surfing* (on Ted's list) would mean different things to someone on a board on the ocean and someone sitting on a couch with a television remote control. Likewise, students see multiple meanings for *dish* and *cable*. Students become responsible for making the transparencies, and soon the focus becomes coming up with a word that will stump everyone. After the banners have been made, students begin looking for words in their textbooks that change meaning when the context changes. Usually by midyear, students begin to comment that "lots and lots of words can mean lots and lots of things." After students have been doing Words Across Contexts for a few weeks, introduce them to context clues.

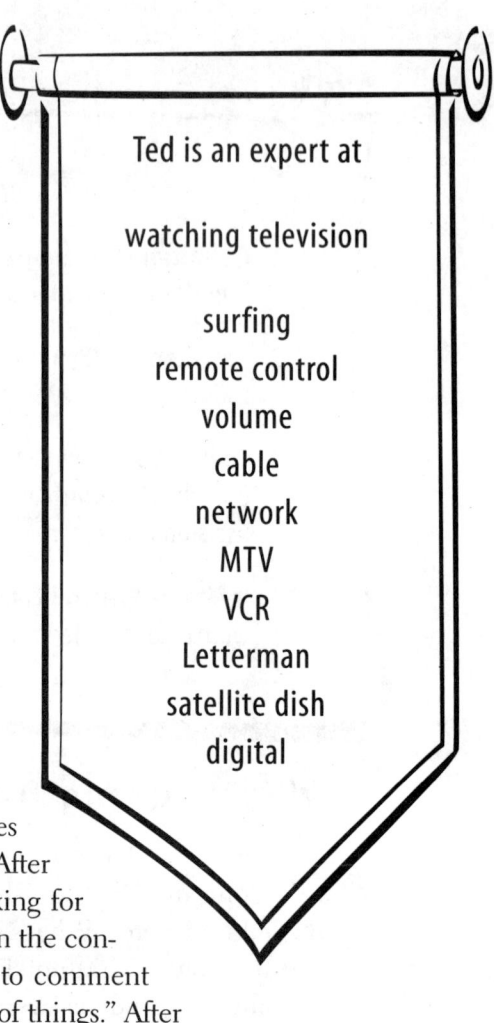

Ted is an expert at

watching television

surfing
remote control
volume
cable
network
MTV
VCR
Letterman
satellite dish
digital

Context Clues, of course, is not a new strategy. Most students have been told for years to use the context clues in a sentence to help them figure out what an unfamiliar word means, but many don't know how to find the clues. One day, years ago, I told a student to do just that when he asked me what the word *verdant* meant in the sentence, "The small group wandered over the verdant hill."

"Use your context clues," I responded.

"What clue?" he asked.

"The clue in the sentence," I replied, still not catching on that the sentence didn't offer a contextual clue for *verdant*.

"Just which clue would that be?" this puzzled student asked.

Then I finally looked. "Oh, no clues," I responded. "It means green."

VOCABULARY DEVELOPMENT STRATEGIES

"Oh," the student said, and he started back to his seat. Then he returned. "You know those clues you were talking about?" he asked. "Well, just what are those clues, anyway?"

Many students have never been taught how to find context clues or even how to determine whether there *are* context clues for an unfamiliar word. Teaching readers how to recognize specific types of context clues and words that signal these clues will help them become more skilled at inferring a word's meaning from its context.

Definition/Explanation clues actually define or explain the unfamiliar word in the same sentence in which the word appears. In the sentence, "A *symbol* is something that stands for something else," the reader learns what the word *symbol* means simply by reading the sentence.

Restatement/Synonym clues explain the unfamiliar word in the text by restating it in simpler terms or by using a synonym. This type of clue is often used in content area textbooks. The following is an example of a restatement clue: "Cowboys wore *chaps*, leather trousers without a seat, over their pants to protect their legs from thorns." Synonym clues can be separated from the unfamiliar word by several other words, as in the sentence, "The food was so *bland* that everyone called it tasteless." Both Restatement/Synonym clues and Antonym clues are often accompanied by signal words. *Signal words* alert you that some sort of affirmation or contrast is coming up—that something is either staying the same or is about to change. If students learn these words and what they signal, they gain insight into unknown words.

Common Signal Words

Restatement/Synonym:
for example
especially
such as
in that
likewise
these

Contrast/Antonym:
by contrast
but
however
although
still
not
despite
some ..., but others
on the other hand

Contrast/Antonym clues offer an opposite meaning for an unfamiliar word. The following is an example of an antonym clue: "Chad is calm and quiet, but his brother is usually *boisterous*." The signal word *but* tells the reader that the opposite of "calm and quiet" is about to appear.

Inference/General Context clues are more subtle than other types of clues. The reader infers the meaning of an unfamiliar word from its general context by determining the relationship between the word and other information in

VOCABULARY DEVELOPMENT STRATEGIES

the text. Inference/General Context clues may be found in the words immediately surrounding the unfamiliar word or in the surrounding sentences. You may even find a clue to the meaning of the word several paragraphs later in the passage. The following sentence is an example of an inference clue: "John burst out of the woods and found himself at the edge of a *precipice*. Clinging to a boulder, he gazed down dizzily at the blue ribbon of river below." The word *precipice* isn't defined, and no synonyms or antonyms are offered. You can, however, figure out what the word means by reading the passage and thinking about the other information in the text: John is at the edge of a rocky, very high place.

As students pay more and more attention to context clues, they will discover that sometimes clues just aren't there. In that case, information about the word's meaning must come directly from the word. Therefore, they need to know something about the meaning of prefixes, suffixes, and root words. With that information, students can often make an intelligent guess about a word's meaning. Studying etymology isn't new; what *is* new is studying it using a vocabulary tree.

Vocabulary Trees require students to not only learn the meaning of a root word or affix, but also recognize that word in different contexts, use it, and listen for it. If we want students really to take ownership of the root word they are learning, they must be able to do more with the word than just memorize it for a multiple-choice exam. Instead, they must look for the word as they read, listen for it in conversation, and use it in their own writing.

You choose the root word (or prefix or suffix) to be studied. (See pages 135–137 for a list of common Greek and Latin roots and affixes.) Students write that word on the root section of the tree. In the trunk section, they write the key word they are learning that contains that root or affix. In the branches, students write other words they discover that have the same root or affix, then go on to create twigs that say where they have heard, seen, and written each word. (See the example of a vocabulary tree on page 128.)

> *If we want students really to take ownership of the root word they are learning, they must be able to do more with the word than just memorize it for a multiple-choice exam.*

None of these strategies is enough for struggling readers, but when combined with the single most effective strategy—reading aloud—they become important tools for students to use to expand their vocabularies.

VOCABULARY DEVELOPMENT STRATEGIES

A Few Questions...

1. **How long do students have to complete a vocabulary tree for each word?**
   Think about having students learn ten to twenty root words really well throughout the school year. That will determine how long students spend on a single vocabulary tree.

2. **Can students work on more than one tree at a time?**
   Yes! In fact, most teachers who use vocabulary trees with students encourage the students to keep working on their trees for very long periods of time. The longer students work on the trees, the more branches and twigs they create.

3. **Should students work on vocabulary trees and context clues at the same time?**
   Again—yes! Vocabulary development must be constant and ongoing. It can't happen with only certain texts on only certain days at only certain times. Students need to be thinking about words and their meanings at all times. Therefore, they need multiple strategies that help them look at words in multiple ways. That's why I like using Words Across Contexts, Context Clues, and Vocabulary Trees all together.

4. **Where do I get the words for the vocabulary trees?**
   Start by looking at the list of common affixes and Latin and Greek bases (see pages 135–137). Then, look at students' texts or talk with their content area teachers to find out what words are coming up that might give them difficulty. Use what you know about Latin and Greek bases or affixes combined with what students are learning in other classes to help you decide which words to teach and in what order to teach them.

5. **Do I need to do the banners to get words for the Words Across Contexts strategy?**
   No. You can simply discuss some examples of multiple-meaning words with students and then have them start looking for words. If you aren't going to use the banner approach, you might consider reading aloud to them Fred Gwynne's wonderful books, *A Chocolate Moose for Dinner* and *The King Who Rained*. These books show words or phrases being used in a context that changes their meaning entirely.

VOCABULARY DEVELOPMENT STRATEGIES

References

Center for the Study of Readers (CSR). 1985. *Becoming a Nation of Readers: The Report of the Commission on Reading.* Washington, D.C.: Center for the Study of Readers.

Gwynne, Fred. 1989. *A Chocolate Moose for Dinner.* New York: Simon & Schuster.

_____. 1989. *The King Who Rained.* New York: Simon & Schuster.

Hill, Margaret. 1998. Reaching Struggling Readers. In *Into Focus: Understanding and Creating Middle School Readers.* Ed. Kylene Beers and Barbara J. Samuels. Norwood, Mass.: Christopher-Gordon Publishers.

Vocabulary Development at a Glance

- **Words Across Contexts:** Students create banners listing ten words related to their "area of expertise," then discuss words on their banners that could mean different things in different contexts.

- **Context Clues:** The teacher explains and discusses the four types of context clues (Definition/Explanation, Restatement/Synonym, Contrast/Antonym, and Inference/General Context) and the words that signal them (such as *especially, however,* and *but*).

- **Vocabulary Trees:** Students create "trees" for each Greek or Latin root or affix they study, filling in branches and twigs with words that use the root or affix and descriptions of where they encountered them.

SOME COMMON ROOTS, PREFIXES, AND SUFFIXES (HILL 1998)

Root Words

	Meaning	Examples
act	do	action, actor, react, transact, enact
aud	hear	audience, auditorium, audible, audition
cred	believe	credit, discredit, incredible, credulous
dic	speak	dictate, predict, contradict, verdict, diction
graph	write	autograph, paragraph, phonograph, photograph, telegraph
loc	place	allocate, dislocate, locate, location
man	hand	manual, manufacture, manuscript, manipulate
mot	move	demote, motion, motor, promote
ped	foot	pedal, pedestrian, pedestal
pop	people	population, popular, populace
port	carry	import, export, portable, porter, transport
sign	mark	insignia, signal, significant, signature
spec	see	inspect, respect, spectacle, spectator, suspect
tract	pull, drag	attract, detract, contract, subtract, traction, tractor
vid	see	evidence, video, provide, providence
volve	roll	evolve, involve, revolve, revolver, revolution

ELEMENTS OF LITERATURE

SOME COMMON ROOTS, PREFIXES, AND SUFFIXES *(cont'd)*

Prefixes

	Meaning	Examples
ad–	to	adapt, add, addict, adhere, admit
amphi–	both, around	amphibian, amphitheater
an–	not	anarchy, anesthesia, anorexia, anonymous
auto–	self	automobile, automatic, autograph, autobiography
co–	together	coauthor, cognate, coincide, cooperate, coordinate
de–	opposite	deactivate, deform, degrade, deplete, descend
dis–	opposite	disagree, disarm, discontinue, disgust, dishonest
for–	not	forbid, forget, forgo
il–	not	illegal, illegible, illegitimate, illiterate, illogical
im–	into	immediate, immerse, immigrate, implant, import
im–	not	imbalance, immaculate, immature, immobilize, impossible
in–	not	inaccurate, inactive, inadvertent, incognito, indecisive
ir–	not	irregular, irreconcilable, irredeemable, irregular, irresponsible
mal–	bad	maladjusted, malaise, malevolent, malfunction, malice
pro–	before	prognosis, progeny, program, prologue, prophet
pro–	forward	proceed, produce, proficient, progress, project
re–	again	redo, rewrite, reappear, repaint, relive
re–	back	recall, recede, reflect, repay, retract
sub–	under	subcontract, subject, submarine, submerge, subordinate, subterranean
trans–	across	transatlantic, transcend, transcribe, transfer, translate
un–	not	unable, uncomfortable, uncertain, unhappy

SOME COMMON ROOTS, PREFIXES, AND SUFFIXES (cont'd)

Suffixes

	Meaning	Examples
–ade	action or process	blockade, escapade, parade
–age	action or process	marriage, pilgrimage, voyage
–ant	one who	assistant, immigrant, merchant, servant
–cle	small	corpuscle, cubicle, particle
–dom	state or quality of	boredom, freedom, martyrdom, wisdom
–ent	one who	dependent, resident, regent, superintendent
–ful	full of	careful, fearful, joyful, thoughtful
–ic	relating to	comic, historic, poetic, public
–less	without	ageless, careless, thoughtless, tireless
–let	small	islet, leaflet, owlet, rivulet, starlet
–ly	resembling	fatherly, motherly, scholarly
–ly	every	daily, weekly, monthly, yearly
–ment	action or process	development, embezzlement, government
–ment	state or quality of	amusement, amazement, predicament
–ment	product or thing	fragment, instrument, ornament
–or	one who	actor, auditor, doctor, donor

READING STRATEGIES AT A GLANCE

Anticipation Guides

- The teacher writes the Anticipation Guide, a set of generalizations based on issues in the text and designed to promote discussion and predictions about the text.
- Students mark whether they agree or disagree with each statement, then discuss their responses.
- While students read, they take notes on the issues in the guide as those issues are revealed in the text.
- After reading, students look at their responses again to see whether they still agree or disagree with each statement.

It Says . . . I Say

- The teacher creates a model It Says . . . I Say chart for the classroom. The chart consists of four columns in which students write a question that requires an inference, what the text says about the question (*It Says*), what they already know about that information (*I Say*), and their inference (*And So*).
- The teacher models the strategy using an inferential question based on a familiar story.
- Students practice making inferences by regularly explaining their answers to inferential questions.

Most Important Word

- After reading a text, students discuss their responses.
- Students decide either independently or in small groups what they think the most important word in the text is, basing their answers on evidence from the text.
- Students share and explain their choices.

READING STRATEGIES AT A GLANCE

Probable Passage

- The teacher chooses key words or phrases from the text students will read, then develops categories for the words and writes the Probable Passage.

- Before students read the text, they arrange the key words and phrases in the categories. Then, they fill in the blanks in the Probable Passage with the key words.

- After students read the text, they discuss how their Probable Passages were similar to or different from the actual text.

Retellings

- The teacher models the Retellings strategy by reading a brief story and retelling it to students. Then, the class evaluates and discusses the teacher's retelling using a Retellings rubric.

- Using the Retellings rubric, students plan and evaluate their retellings.

- The teacher assesses students' progress over time by plotting their scores on a chart.

Save the Last Word for Me

- After reading a text, students prepare a Last Word card, writing their favorite passage from the text on the front of the card and why they liked it on the back.

- In small groups, students take turns reading the quotations on their cards, allowing other members of the group to respond, and then reading their "last words" from the back of the card.

Say Something

- The teacher models the strategy by "saying something" about a text with a colleague or by reading and discussing a typed Say Something dialogue with students.

- Students read a short text, stopping occasionally to discuss the text with a partner. In their conversations, students must make a prediction, ask a question, make a comment, or make a connection.

- Students practice Say Somethings using very short texts before using the strategy with assignments.

READING STRATEGIES AT A GLANCE

Scales

- The teacher chooses and writes a scale based on the desired learning objective (for example, comparing two characters in a story). Students complete a Likert Scale to respond to generalizations about the story, a Semantic Differential Scale to analyze characters, or a Comparison Grid to compare characters from different stories.
- After reading a text, students complete the scale, explaining their choices using specific evidence from the text.
- Students share their responses in a small-group discussion, debate, or other activity.

Sketch to Stretch

- The teacher introduces Sketch to Stretch to students by showing and discussing symbolic pictures based on a text.
- After reading a selection, students work independently or with a partner to create symbolic sketches of their interpretations of the text. On the back of their sketches, students write why they drew what they did, using evidence from the text to support their opinions.
- Students share their sketches in small groups, allowing other students to comment before revealing their explanations of their sketches.

Somebody Wanted But So

- After students read a story, they work alone or in groups to fill in columns on the Somebody Wanted But So chart: who the *Somebody* in a story is, what he or she *Wanted*, *But* what happened that created a problem, and *So* how the problem was resolved. Students join statements with the word *then* when needed.
- Students work together to condense SWBS statements into concise summaries or to develop summaries for long texts such as novels.
- To focus on literary elements, students can write SWBS statements for different characters in the same story or for different types of conflicts.

Story Impressions

- The teacher chooses key words or phrases from the story students are going to read and arranges them in a linked order.

ELEMENTS OF LITERATURE

READING STRATEGIES AT A GLANCE

- The class discusses the words' pronunciations and meanings.
- Using all the key words or phrases in the order they were given, students write brief summaries of what they think the story will be about.
- After reading, students compare their predictions with the actual story.

Text Reformulation

- The teacher introduces Text Reformulation by having students reformulate a text they have read into a patterned story, such as an If/Then or ABC story.
- The teacher models several types of reformulations.
- Either the teacher or the students choose which type of reformulation to do based on the desired learning objective.

Think-Aloud

- The teacher models a Think-Aloud for students, letting them tally on the Think-Aloud tally sheet the types of comments the teacher makes (predicting, picturing the text, comparing, identifying a problem, or fixing up a problem).
- Students practice the strategy with a partner using short and easy texts before using Think-Aloud with their assignments.
- Students regularly practice Think-Alouds, eventually using them on their own as needed.

Vocabulary Development

- **Words Across Contexts:** Students create banners listing ten words related to their "area of expertise," then discuss words on their banners that could mean different things in different contexts.
- **Context Clues:** The teacher explains and discusses the four types of context clues (Definition/Explanation, Restatement/Synonym, Contrast/Antonym, and Inference/General Context) and the words that signal them (such as *especially*, *however*, and *but*).
- **Vocabulary Trees:** Students create "trees" for each Greek or Latin root or affix they study, filling in branches and twigs with words that use the root or affix and descriptions of where they encountered them.

BIBLIOGRAPHY

Bleich, David. 1975. *Reading and Feelings: An Introduction to Subjective Criticism.* Urbana, Illinois: National Council of Teachers of English.

Brown, Hazel, and Brian Cambourne. 1990. *Read and Retell.* Portsmouth, N.H.: Heinemann Publishers.

Center for the Study of Readers (CSR). 1985. *Becoming a Nation of Readers: The Report of the Commission on Reading.* Washington, D.C.: Center for the Study of Readers.

Davey, Beth. 1983. Think-Aloud: Modeling the Cognitive Processes of Reading Comprehension. *Journal of Reading* 27:44–47.

Feathers, Karen. 1993. *InfoText.* Portsmouth, N.H.: Heinemann Publishers.

Harste, Jerome C., Kathy Gnagey Short, and Carolyn L. Burke. 1988. *Creating Classrooms for Authors: The Reading-Writing Connection.* Portsmouth, N.H.: Heinemann Publishers.

Hill, Margaret. 1998. Reaching Struggling Readers. In *Into Focus: Understanding and Creating Middle School Readers.* Edited by Kylene Beers and Barbara Samuels. Norwood, Mass.: Christopher-Gordon Publishers.

Johnson, Terry D., and Daphne R. Louis. 1987. *Literacy through Literature.* Portsmouth, N.H.: Heinemann Publishers.

MacOn, James M., Diane Bewell, and Maryellen Vogt. 1991. *Responses to Literature.* Newark, Del.: International Reading Association.

McGinley, William J., and Peter R. Denner. 1987. Story Impressions: A Prereading/Writing Activity. *Journal of Reading* 31:248–253.

Olshavsky, Jill Edwards. 1976–77. Reading as Problem-Solving: An Investigation of Strategies. *Reading Research Quarterly* 12:654–674.

Raphael, Taffy. 1982. Question-Answering Strategies for Children. *The Reading Teacher* 36:186–190.

Short, Kathy Gnagey, Jerome C. Harste, and Carolyn L. Burke. 1996. *Creating Classrooms for Authors and Inquirers.* 2d ed. Portsmouth, N.H.: Heinemann Publishers.

Tierney, Robert J., John E. Readence, and Ernest K. Dishner. 1995. *Reading Strategies and Practices: A Compendium.* 4th ed. Needham Heights, Mass.: Allyn & Bacon.

Wallis, John. 1998. Strategies: What Connects Readers to Meaning. In *Into Focus: Understanding and Creating Middle School Readers,* edited by Kylene Beers and Barbara J. Samuels. Norwood, Mass.: Christopher-Gordon Publishers.

Wood, Karen. 1984. Probable Passages: A Writing Strategy. *The Reading Teacher* 37:496–499.